The Missing Element in Church Development

The Missing Element in Church Development

by

Dr. Paul E. Paino

Paul E. Paino Ministries, Inc.
P.O. Box 12205
Fort Wayne, Indiana USA 46863-2205

FOREWORD

REVIVAL is the result of a sovereign act of God. Man cannot produce or promote a genuine outpouring of the Spirit. We can pray and we can commit ourselves to a life of righteousness and separation but only the Holy Spirit can give REVIVAL.

EVANGELISM is the result of a vision, a burden, and a plan to witness to the lost. The church has been commanded to **EVANGELIZE**. The "Great Commission" is a mandate from our Lord to "go into all the world and preach the gospel." This is our responsibility.

CHURCH GROWTH is the result of work, planning, and structure. Great preaching alone does not build great churches. A church can be blessed with members who are dedicated to earnest prayer. However, praying alone does not build great churches. Programs and promotion can produce great crowds. The people will become spectators. But programs by themselves will not produce great churches.

CHURCH GROWTH is the result of carefully laid plans. Churches grow when people are involved, when organization and structure are put into place; and when people are challenged to use their giftings and talents for the work of the Lord. Behind every strong and growing church, there is a solid foundation, a framework, or skeleton that holds the "body" together as it reaches out in its ministry.

For the past many years I have studied the organization and structure of the church. It is clearly set forth in the New Testament; and, as churches follow the pattern, growth is inevitable. It is my desire in the following pages to share some insight with the reader with the prayer that more churches will multiply and grow for the glory of God!!

ACKNOWLEDGEMENTS

For the past 25 years I have had the desire to put into writing material that I have gleaned that has assisted in the building of several strong churches. This task could not have been completed without the assistance of several people.

First, I wish to thank my staff of workers and teachers who have helped me prepare and implement the programs that are laid out in this book. I am especially grateful to Rev. Scott Mills, our Youth Pastor, for his input.

It is appropriate that I thank my secretary, Ann Liechty, for the many hours she put into typing and preparing the manuscript. This was done under a great deal of pressure and was accomplished because of sacrificial work.

As I have traveled across the nation, hundreds of pastors have requested that the information I share in seminars would be put in writing. As a result of these requests, I have attemptcd to do so.

For the past 25 years I have been working on a set of manuals that provides all of the Sunday School lessons for every grade level of the church. These manuals also provide schedules, promotional programs, illustrations, student profiles, and much other material that makes it possible for a church to operate a successful School of the Bible program. Once this material is purchased, there is never a need to invest any more money. The program is complete.

If you have any questions concerning these manuals, please feel free to contact my office.

Dr. Paul E. Paino

CONTENTS

CHAPTER ONE

STRUCTURE THE MISSING ELEMENT

PREACHING

In attendance, churches reach plateaus! When reading the book of Acts, we discover that there are certain elements that must be present if a New Testament church is to be established. Without properly developing these elements in the local assembly, there will be no sustained growth.

The early church was characterized by powerful and persuasive preaching. The response to the preaching of Peter in Acts chapter 2 resulted in 3,000 members being added to the church. The Apostle Paul, along with his traveling partners, went from city to city and preached and taught the Word of God. As a result, churches were established throughout Asia, Asia-Minor, and Europe.

During the persecution in Jerusalem, the disciples scattered and *"they went everywhere preaching the gospel."*

No Christian church can be established unless the Word of God is preached and taught. The command of Jesus must be obeyed. **"Go into all the world and preach the gospel."** Jesus made the promise, "upon this Rock I will build my church and the gates of hell shall not prevail against it." As the gospel is preached, churches will be established. ***THIS IS THE FIRST PREREQUISITE TO BUILDING A CHURCH.*** The Word must be preached! It takes Bible preaching to build strong churches!

PRAYING

Churches are established, sustained, and grow when members of the local church pray. Just as preaching is a prerequisite, so is praying. It is said concerning the believers in the Jerusalem church;

> *"And they continued steadfastly in the apostles' doctrine and fellowship, and in breaking of bread, and in prayers."*
>
> *Acts 2:42*

They continued daily with one accord in the temple. As the church prayed and praised God, there was increase daily in the fellowship.

> *"And, the Lord added to the church daily such as should be saved."*
>
> *Acts 2:47*

When the early believers came under strong persecution and Peter and John were cast into prison, the Bible says concerning them;

> *"And when they heard that, <u>they lifted up their voice to God</u> with one accord, and said, Lord, thou art God, which hast made heaven, and earth, and the sea, and all that in them is."*
>
> *Acts 4:24*

The church learned early the necessity of PRAYER. The moment a congregation is born, opposition will arise. There are great spiritual forces that are determined to thwart the increase in the Body of Christ. It was true in the early church, and it is true today. The only way that an infant congregation can survive and grow is when the believers are willing to meet **"in one accord"** and earnestly pray.

The early church was threatened, and it appeared that the church would be destroyed. However, we read in the record,

> *"And when they had prayed, the place was shaken where they were assembled together; and they were all filled with the Holy Ghost, and they spake the word of God with boldness."*
>
> *Acts 4:31*

<u>The church prayed earnestly</u>, the church prayed for boldness to witness, <u>the church prayed</u> in one accord, <u>the church prayed</u> for power, and the church grew. The church today cannot grow unless the Word

is preached. And the church will be destroyed if believers in the church do not pray.

Over the years, I have seen tremendous things take place in the church that I pastor as a result of the prayers of God's people. Every Saturday night for over 50 years we have had "an hour of prayer." God has blessed the church with a group of "praying women" who meet every morning for a time of intercessory prayer. A group of men meet at the church daily at 6:00 a.m. to seek the Lord. I made a commitment that we would never close a church service without asking people to spend time in earnest prayer around our altars.

God has raised up individuals who have felt called to pray for the church and for my ministry. I am convinced that we have experienced growth and blessing because of this "spirit of prayer."

SIGNS AND WONDERS

Churches grow when the **MIRACULOUS** is present!! The church is a "spiritual body" and the power of the Holy Spirit must be present. The early believers prayed for "signs and wonders." They prayed in *Acts 4:29 and 30,*

> *"And now, Lord, behold their threatenings: and grant unto thy servants, that with all boldness they may speak thy word, by stretching forth thine hand to heal; and that signs and wonders may be done by the name of thy holy child Jesus."*

They believed in the *SUPERNATURAL!* They expected and depended upon the miraculous. In Acts 5, verses 12 through 16, the Lord was present to heal. There was deliverance from devils and the powers of darkness. The testimony was: **"they were healed every one."** The supernatural attracted the people. The miraculous provided deliverance from oppression, fear, and bondage.

Today if the church is going to grow, the supernatural and the miraculous must be present. When the Word of God is preached in the power and the demonstration of the Holy Spirit, believers will be added to the Body. If this element is missing, the church will never be able to accomplish all God intends for it to accomplish. So, the prerequisites for growth are *GREAT PREACHING, GREAT PRAYING, AND GREAT POWER.*

"But ye shall receive power, after that the Holy Ghost is come upon you; and ye shall be witnesses unto me both in Jerusalem, and in all Judaea, and in Samaria, and unto the uttermost part of the earth."
Acts 1:8

CONSECRATION AND COMMITMENT

When the Apostle Luke wrote the book of Acts, he carefully describes how members of the early church sold what they did not need and laid their gifts at the apostles' feet. They were not instructed to do so. There was no evidence this was expected of them. It was a result of a deep desire in their hearts to be totally surrendered to the work of the ministry. There was great unity in the Body as each one participated. This consecration and **"oneness of spirit"** released tremendous power in the church. They were with **"one accord"** in the upper room, they were in "one accord" when they prayed for boldness and signs and wonders, and they were in "one accord" and **one mind** when they sold land and property and brought the money before the apostles. This consecration and this unity resulted in the church increasing miraculously.

A few years ago, when challenging the congregation to enter into a building program, there arose a handful of people who decided to oppose the vision and the work. It was the result of one person taking a stand against the program. In a matter of days the opposition grew and a spirit of division prevailed. During the process, members left the church. It appeared that the work of God would be destroyed. For the first time in the history of the church you could sense oppression and division. It was a dark time. The unity of the Spirit was broken. No longer was the Body *"in one accord."* It was a sad time. We went through difficult days.

It took three years to recover from this time of ***broken unity.*** The church is never weakened when it is opposed and hindered by outside forces. The church is devastated when unity is broken within the Body. No church can grow when a divisive spirit prevails. In the early church, the Holy Spirit intervened and brought death to Ananias and Sapphira because they broke the unity that was in the "Body" and lied to the Holy Spirit.

It was Ananias and Sapphira who compromised the commitment and destroyed the unity in the Body. They "lied to the Holy Ghost." Their consecration was incomplete. They identified with the church, but they were not in unity with the church. The breaking of this consecration was so critical that the Holy Spirit struck a death blow to the hypocrisy. There must be a sacrificial commitment. There must be a unity of spirit. Believers must stay in "one accord." If this is not done, the local church will suffer and death will overtake it.

As a result of the Holy Spirit's intervention into this compromise, we read,

> ***"And great fear came upon all the church, and upon as many as heard these things."***
>
> ***Acts 5:11***

It brought a godly reverence among the people. Believers were the more added to the Lord, and the church continued to grow.

The greatest problem that we have in increasing our churches today is the lack of consecration, commitment, sacrifice, and unity. Too many are not faithful with their tithe and their offerings. When God's people are faithful to give, God is faithful to bless. It is true in the local church.

It has been thrilling to see how people have responded to the work of the Lord. A few years ago, a man came to our Conference Grounds and was gloriously saved. He owned a trucking firm. The Lord had blessed him financially. Because he was so thrilled that the Lord had changed his life, he purchased an insurance policy and made the church the irrevocable beneficiary. After his death, the church received a check for $1,240,000. This man blessed the Kingdom of God.

When we started our building program, two of the families in our church, who own businesses, made commitments to the Lord. They each pledged $1,000,000 to the work of the ministry. God used people like this to help "the Body" accomplish great things for the Lord.

The Lord has raised up hundreds of faithful people who work faithfully, pay their tithes, give sacrificial offerings, and make their talents available to the Lord.

<u>Consecration and commitment is a prerequisite to church growth.</u>

When each member of the church recognizes that the Lord has given to them a special and particular ministry gift; and, when they are willing to use it, the church will grow.

LEADERSHIP

Jesus spent His entire earthly ministry preparing leadership for the church. Without Apostolic leaders the church will not grow. The Apostle Paul wrote to the church at Ephesus and explained the divine order of leadership.

> *"He that descended is the same also that ascended up far above all heavens, that he might fill all things. <u>And he gave some, apostles; and some, prophets; and some, evangelists; and some, pastors and teachers;</u> For the perfecting of the saints,*

for the work of the ministry, for the edifying of the body of Christ: Till we all come in the unity of the faith, and of the knowledge of the Son of God, unto a perfect man, unto the measure of the stature of the fullness of Christ.

Ephesians 4:10-13

Apostles, prophets, evangelists, preachers, and teachers are placed in the church to give leadership to the church!! Leadership does not come from the pew. Leadership must come from the pulpit. In *Acts chapter 6, verse 2,* we read,

"Then the twelve called the multitude of the disciples unto them, and said, It is not reason that we should leave the word of God, and serve tables."

The twelve disciples gave direction to the church! It was they who pointed the church in the right direction. Leadership that does not have a plan, a word from the Lord, or a sense of direction will not lead a church into expansion and growth.

The Apostle Paul gave instruction to Timothy.

"And the things that thou hast heard of me among many witnesses, the same commit thou to faithful men, who shall be able to teach others also."

II Timothy 2:2

Leadership must train! Leadership must teach and instruct. Leadership must point the way. Leadership must involve others. Without strong leadership, the church will not prosper and grow.

LEADERSHIP QUALITIES

There are some basic qualities that must be found in godly leaders:

(1) A LEADER MUST HAVE A CONSECRATED LIFE (Romans 12:1-2). Unless a leader is totally committed to the task of leadership, he will not be successful. Too many potential leaders are diverted away from the task by other secular activities. There must be a near-fanatic commitment to the work.

(2) A LEADER MUST POSSESS SPIRITUAL VISION. The Apostle Paul had insight. His vision was not clouded but very clear. He knew what was required of him. He knew where he was going, and he knew what he was to do.

Vision and compassion go hand in hand. Jesus said to his disciples, "Lift up your eyes and look on the fields." It was further stated of him, "He was moved with compassion." Men and woman who have vision will be leaders.

(3) A LEADER MUST BE FAITHFUL (Hebrews 10:24-25). "It is required of a steward that he be found faithful." I have seen many, many people over the years that God wanted to use in a special way. But, they were not faithful. Unless we are faithful in the

little things, God cannot trust us to handle important matters.

(4) *A LEADER MUST BE A TITHER.* Pastors and ministers need to find a place to designate their tithing outside of their own ministry. The blessing of the Lord cannot rest on a leader who is not faithful in financial matters.

(5) *A LEADER MUST POSSESS "A MISSIONARY SPIRIT."* The moment a leader directs the church into world evangelism and to the fulfillment of "The Great Commission," God's blessing will be poured out. The command of Jesus was for us to go into all the world. We are to minister not only in our Jerusalem but "to the uttermost part of the earth."

(6) *A LEADER MUST BE WILLING TO COOPERATE WITH OTHER WORKERS* (Exodus 17:11-13). When the Amalekites were warring against Israel, Joshua led the forces to battle. Aaron and Hur stood beside Moses and held up his hands. As these ***leaders worked together,*** God gave the victory.

(7) *A LEADER MUST BE OPEN, HONEST, AND TRANSPARENT* (Acts 6:3). God wants us to be men and women of "honest report." There is no place for professionalism or insincerity. Sooner or later flaws in character will manifest themselves. A leader cannot hide. God blesses the person who is open and honest and willing to confess and repent when they have failed (Psalm 51).

(8) *A LEADER MUST BE FULL OF THE HOLY GHOST.* One of the first requirements that was made by the apostles concerning the seven deacons that were chosen was that they must be "men of honest report, **FULL OF THE HOLY GHOST.**" Stephen was a man "full of faith and of the Holy Spirit." When we are filled with the Spirit of God, we manifest the character of Christ. This makes true leaders.

STRUCTURE

A congregation can be blessed with a capable preacher-teacher. Members of the church can respond to the call to pray. Believers can be faithful in their giving and willingness to labor and work; and, the Lord can bless and confirm the Word by healing and delivering people. But, unless careful thought is given to the ***STRUCTURE OF THE LOCAL CHURCH,*** growth cannot be sustained.

Acts 6:1 says,

> ***"And in those days, when the number of the disciples was multiplied, there arose a murmuring of the Grecians against the Hebrews, because their widows were neglected in the daily ministration."***

You will notice that there was great increase in the church. Along with the ***MULTIPLICATION*** of members there arose a ***MURMURING*** from the members. Increase in the number of people produces an increase in problems.

When the twelve disciples became aware of the problem, they knew that something very practical had to be done or the problems that were arising would devastate the Body. So, special care was given. ***THE APOSTLES LED THE CHURCH INTO ORGANIZATIONAL STRUCTURE.***

The leadership knew that they must not be diverted away from prayer and the ministry of the Word. ***IT WAS TIME TO ORGANIZE!!!*** It was necessary to put structure into the church.

The increase in membership put demands upon the church to meet the needs of the people. It was impossible for leadership to meet these needs by their preaching alone. They had to have help. Others must be involved. A plan needed to be laid out. So, increase in people produced an increase in problems, and the increase in problems made it necessary to involve the people so the problems could be met. The disciples said,

> ***"Wherefore, brethren, look ye out among you seven men of honest report, full of the Holy Ghost and wisdom, whom we may appoint over this business. But we will give ourselves continually to prayer, and to the ministry of the word."***
>
> ***Acts 6:3-4***

The early church responded to this direction and the whole church was pleased with the plan. Out of this situation deacons were "appointed" to the responsibility of meeting the needs of the church. Deacons were set aside ***TO SERVE.*** They were not to be rulers or controllers.

Deacons must learn that they are ordained to protect the pastor. They must discover ***his vision!!*** They must know the pastor's heart. A deacon must be prepared to defend leadership, its ministry, and its program.

Deacons were used so that pastors could give themselves to prayer and the teaching of the Word. Deacons are to minister to needs, solve problems, and stand strongly behind the pastor so the work of the ministry can be accomplished.

Deacons are not to make themselves available so that the people can feel free to criticize, find fault, or hinder the work of the Lord. The deacon is to stand shoulder to shoulder with the pastor and lift from his shoulders anything that will keep him from his calling in ministering the Word.

The problem arose among the Hellenistic widows, and the early church appointed spirit-filled Greek members to minister to the need. When needs arise in the church, the people who have the needs should be involved in solving the problems. This was the beginning of ***STRUCTURE*** in the early church. Organizational plans gave the church a track upon which it could run. Structure involves more people. Every believer is endowed with a ministry gift.

> ***"For as we have many members in one body, and <u>all members have not the same office:</u> So we, being many, are one body in Christ, and every one members one of another. <u>Having then gifts</u> differing according to the grace that is given to us, whether prophecy, let us prophesy according to the proportion of faith; Or ministry, let us***

wait on our ministering: or he that teacheth, on teaching; Or he that exhorteth, on exhortation; he that giveth, let him do it with simplicity; he that ruleth, with diligence; he that sheweth mercy, with cheerfulness."

Romans 12:4-8

Without this involvement, church growth cannot be maintained.

Churches reach plateaus. Seventy percent of the evangelical churches in America run under 100 in attendance. This will never change until something positive is done concerning involving people in "the work of the ministry." There is a reason why so many churches never grow past the 100 mark. They are stopped on this first plateau. The next plateau is 250, then 500, then 1,000 and over. Each plateau has its own characteristics. There are reasons why a church cannot grow from one level to the next.

GOD WANTS TO GIVE INCREASE!!!

The church of the Lord Jesus Christ must multiply. We have a world to reach for Christ.

I want to address some of the reasons why churches are not moving from one plateau to the next. It is the purpose of this book to share suggestions so that churches can grow. The Lord is interested in addition and multiplication. When we are willing to cultivate, sow, and water, **THE LORD WILL GIVE AN INCREASE.**

CHAPTER TWO

STRUCTURE
HOW TO ATTAIN IT

Churches cannot grow beyond their foundation. When the local assembly is not properly organized, it cannot sustain the growth that comes to it. Many, many churches experience increase and then become frustrated when they are unable to hold the increase for any appreciative time.

Please note the following illustration:

I call your attention to item "A" in the illustration. This represents the foundation of the local church.

If the foundation will support 50-100 people, the church will never grow any larger than the foundation (structure). If the foundation "A" is properly laid to support 200-250, that will be the size of the church. A church will never grow in numerical attendance beyond what the foundation (structure) will support.

If during a period of spiritual refreshing God sends people into the congregation, the church will experience a temporary growth. This growth is illustrated by letter"C" in the drawing.

Now, the moment this increase comes, if the foundation is not expanded, "D," to support the increase, the new people will become SPECTATORS. No plan has been made in the structure to involve them and to hold them.

When people remain spectators in a local church for any length of time, they will tend to become criticizers. They are not involved. They do not feel that they are a part. They often feel out of place and rejected and soon become uncomfortable in the local fellowship. If this condition is not corrected immediately after the increase, people will become dissatisfied and they will begin to affect many that have been faithful and involved in the church.

What usually follows is a schism, a breakaway, a division, and broken relationships. Churches all over America will experience a time of growth. Immediately following the growth cycle there will be a breakaway and the attendance of the church will fall back to what the foundation can support.

The early church had simple structure. Then, there arose a problem. Leadership broadened the base and appointed servants to minister to the needs of the people. This was the beginning of structure. Soon, elders were added to the local church. The Apostle Paul began to deal with the necessity of involving each member of the Body of Christ in his or her calling and gift. Everyone had to be involved. There had to be a place for each person to minister. The foundation had to expand in order to support the increase. Unless careful thought is given to the structural base of the local church, the local church will not increase.

The reason that seventy percent of the evangelical churches in America run 100 or less is because the foundation will not support a larger church. The assembly is stopped at this plateau and will never rise any higher until changes are made. This is true with each and every plateau that a church reaches.

As a result of a recent survey of 14,000 churches, it was determined that eighty-five percent of these churches have not had any increase in attendance in the past several years. They are stagnant. They have ceased to grow. There is no increase. Unless serious changes are made, there will be members in the church who will want to be involved in some congregation that is vibrant, growing, and accomplishing something for the Lord.

Often times when they see that this is not going to happen, they transfer to a church that is showing signs of growth and increase. Today ninety percent of the new members that identify with a growing church transfer to the new church from some other church. A very small percentage of most growing churches is a result of new converts. The growth is the result of transferred members.

When people change churches because the gospel is not being preached, doctrine is being compromised, and spiritual truths are not being taught, blessing is brought to the church that they decide to attend. But, when a person leaves a church because they have become offended, they are opposed to some decision that has been made, they do not get the attention they feel they need, or they don't want to assume some responsibility or are resisting some challenge, they contaminate the Body of Christ.

All of our churches have experienced people coming and going who were weakening the Body of Christ and spreading problems and negativism from one congregation to the next. You can never build a church on the "floaters" or "church hoppers." They are a "mixed multitude." When people are willing to fit into the foundation, when they can be incorporated into the basic structure of the church, the church will grow and will be a blessing in the community.

There are many characteristics of a church that runs under 100 in its attendance. Let me list some of these characteristics for you.

(1) This church is usually led by some strong local "lay-person." The pastor is not the true leader. The church is dictated to and controlled by some strong lay-person. This person has this authority because of several reasons, and he is its true leader.

(2) Often the church has a negative testimony in the community.

(3) The small church has a tendency to be a family affair. It's so family oriented that an outsider finds it

difficult to become one of the number. This church tends to be exclusive rather than to be inclusive.

(4) The church usually has at lease two different factions in it. Often these factions are very subtle; however, they are very, very real and powerful.

(5) The small church often has difficulty because of inadequate facilities.

(6) The church is sometimes hindered because of the lack of sufficient talents in music, teachers, and leadership qualities.

(7) This church often suffers from financial problems and difficulties.

(8) The small church can easily develop worship habits that are exclusive.

(9) There is no real vision to make the church any different. People will tend to resist change because their sense of security is disturbed.

(10) Program schedules are not carefully thought through.

(11) The small church can over emphasize some particular doctrinal theme or feel that they must champion some doctrinal statement or position that is not necessary to salvation.

(12) This church has a tendency to become legalistic or demanding.

(13) The pastor has not established an office with regular business hours.

(14) There is resistance to change and the danger to become involved in "religious fads."

(15) There are no realistic goals. This is true in attendance, finances, and programming.

(16) The church is "self" centered. The members are interested in social activity, family activity, and programs that benefit themselves.

(17) The church does not have a proper covering and the pastor is often not accountable to anybody.

(18) There is no program or challenge to reach people on the outside.

(19) The leadership at the church has not taken advantage of the local media.

(20) There is a lack of specific assignments so that the members of the church can be developed and disciplined in areas of ministry.

(21) Not enough time is given to train and teach members how to handle the Word of God.

(22) Because of the lack of goals, there is no way to measure success.

(23) There is a need to formulate a plan to reach the outsider.

(24) The church facilities are not kept clean and inviting.

(25) The church has a reputation of being involved in "extremes."

(26) The church has developed a sense of spiritual superiority, has become judgmental, and sometimes legalistic.

(27) The pastor has not made sufficient effort to make his presence felt in the community outside of the church.

(28) The pastor has no deep sense that God has called him to the church he is pastoring. Many pas-

tors are simply waiting for something better to come along.

(29) The church refuses to respect the pastor as "the man of God." Unless the pastor is respected as the leader and the director of the church, the church will not grow.

(30) Pastors become discouraged before they have established themselves as the leader of the church. A person must pastor a congregation for at least three years before they can truly pastor the people.

(31) Sunday School classes and elective classes are not carefully scheduled.

(32) There is no credibility concerning financial matters.

These characteristics often prevail in the small church; and unless these matters are prayerfully addressed, the church will never grow. A church running around 100 in attendance can become "too cozy." A small church can easily become a clique. It is easy for the church's philosophy to become self-centered. Members feel the church exists for itself and its members. There is very little effort made to reach the lost. Christians are not challenged to be witnesses and to reach out to their neighbors and friends. Evangelism is lost and a wrong emphasis is placed on fellowship.

Many people choose the small church because they want the intimacy and the fellowship and do not care for the burden and the work that is involved in making the church grow. The church can become a social club. Such a church will never impact its community for the cause of Christ. The church is "a fellowship." It is a body. But, the church is more than this. The church has a mandate. We are to be ambassadors and witnesses. We are called to a task. So, fellowship and labor must go hand in hand. One without the other will destroy balance in the body.

Churches must grow under the direction of a motivated, inspired, and strong leader. Churches will grow when lay people are encouraged and challenged to get involved. Churches grow when believers are willing to work. The church needs laborers. We are to become workers together with God.

We read some very interesting words in *Ephesians chapter 4, verses 15 and 16.*

> *"But speaking the truth in love, may grow up into him in all things, which is the head, even Christ; From whom the whole body fitly joined together and compacted by that which every joint supplieth, according to the effectual working in the measure of every part, maketh increase of the body unto the edifying of itself in love."*

We learn that a church grows because of its relationship with "the head, even Christ." To the extent that members of the body relate properly to the Head, there will be increase. When the body is weak and infirm, the church will decline. When members have weak hands and feeble knees and ears that do not hear and eyes that are dim, the church will not grow. There must be a constant union with Christ on the part of each and every member if the church is to grow.

A church will grow when it recognizes that each member is *"...fitly joined together."* Every member must function. Every person must be involved. Each church member must fill his place. When there is harmony, singleness of heart, oneness of purpose, the body is strong. The church is the instrument through which the Holy Spirit reveals the thoughts and purposes of God. When each member is willing to fit into this structure, there will be increase.

A church grows when each member recognizes that we are "...compacted by that which every joint supplieth." Each member of the body has a gift. Each part of the body must function. The body is knit together and each joint must function. It is the responsibility of the ministry gifts of Christ to the church to minister to the church so that every gift can be used.

This is made very clear when the Apostle Paul continues by saying, "...according to the effectual working of *every part*." Every Christian is a vital part in the local body. The Apostle Paul says in *Romans 12:6-8;*

> *"Having then gifts differing according to the grace that is given to us, whether prophecy, let us prophesy according to the proportion of faith; Or ministry, let us wait on our ministering: or he that teacheth, on teaching; Or he that exhorteth, on exhortation: he that giveth, let him do it with simplicity; he that ruleth, with diligence; he that sheweth mercy, with cheerfulness."*

Each person must function in his ministry according to his gifting. A person is blessed when he realizes his part in the body and is willing to give freely to the church so that its ministry may be expanded. When each member of the church ministers, the church becomes strong. When the members are only interested in being ministered to, the church becomes weak.

The church is a living organism. Each member is to receive strength from some other member. *"...maketh increase of the body unto the edification of itself in love."* The body will not increase unless each member edifies other members, To the extent that this is true, the body will increase.

May God grant to all of our churches a renewal in the Holy Spirit so that we can fulfill God's divine plans for the church.

There are things that every person can do to be a help in the local church.

(1) *We must discover and use our spiritual gifts.* The New Testament makes it clear that each and every one has been given a gift. We will be held accountable for the gifts that God has given to us. When a congregation is allowed to be "unemployed," that church cannot grow. Everyone must faithfully use his gifts.

(2) *We all can help the church as we are willing to influence our friends and our relatives.* Statistics declare that between eighty and ninety percent of all first timers to church come because a friend or a relative invites them. It is evident that church growth is largely related to present members inviting their friends and relatives.

(3) *We all must be willing to open our hearts and our fellowship to visitors and new converts.* We must make room for them. They must be warmly accepted.

All too often we shut out the newcomer. We will not go out of our way to be friendly and to invite them into our circle. People are lonely. Many are searching for acceptance. Each member must do his part to create an atmosphere that will make the first timer and the outsider comfortable.

(4) *Every member can help the church grow by exercising a positive faith that growth will happen.* Too many members are without vision. Many have become self-centered, self-satisfied, and self-occupied. Many congregations have difficulty finding Sunday School teachers. Often people with talents will not come forward. There are opportunities on every side for people to be involved. But, there must be a willingness in the hearts of the people.

Jesus is the Master Builder. He said, *"I will build My church."* Jesus wants us to be builders with Him. It is His plan that His Church will grow. We who are members of the Body of Christ can work together with the Lord to build His Church.

SUNDAY SCHOOL IS IMPORTANT

The Sunday School (School of the Bible) can be a God-anointed instrument. There is nothing in the organizational structure of the church that can be as effective, powerful, far-reaching, and all-inclusive as a properly functioning school. The Sunday School (School of the Bible) when properly organized and structured will challenge Christians to be **"workers together with God."**

You will find listed in the following pages 10 very important reasons why a church school program **must be** organized.

(1) ***THE SUNDAY SCHOOL CAN REACH ALL AGES WITH THE GOSPEL*** (Matthew 28:19-20). Only the Sunday School provides the structure and the facility for reaching every age with the Gospel. The Sunday School can break the age barrier, the cultural barrier, the economic barrier, the race barrier, and the denominational barrier!

The pastor or minister of education cannot reach every age in his community. Without a church school program, much of the work of evangelism and gospel teaching would completely miss the largest segment of the population. The church school can reach ALL for Christ. We are commanded and commissioned to preach the gospel so that no one will be omitted. The Sunday School makes it possible.

(2) ***THE SUNDAY SCHOOL MOBILIZES PEOPLE FOR CHRIST.*** (I Corinthians 3:9, 14) "We are laborers together with God." (Matthew 9:37,38) "Pray the Lord of harvest to thrust forth laborers."

Christians want to be involved in God's work. Involved people are faithful people and working people are happy people. Too much attention has been focused on the platform. We are not demanding enough activity from the layman in the pew.

Every Christian knows he should work for Christ. However, not every Christian knows what to do for Christ. The Sunday School affords the church the opportunity to put every available worker busy for

Christ. The Sunday School dictates what can be done for Christ. People work when their work is delegated.

(3) ***THE SUNDAY SCHOOL TRAINS WORKERS*** (I Thessalonians 1:3-7) Christians cannot be effective unless they are taught the truths of God's Word, unless they exercise in prayer and worship. The Sunday School is responsible for training people in the presentation of the gospel. The Sunday School instructs workers to "rightly divide the Word of Truth." (II Timothy 2:15)

The Sunday School trains and instructs Christians in the art of soul-winning, in the necessity of witnessing, in the thrill and blessing of reaching others, and in the necessity for understanding the needs of people. Nothing trains as efficiently as Sunday School.

(4) ***THE SUNDAY SCHOOL IS AN INSTRUMENT FOR REACHING THE UNREACHED.*** Most evangelistic services appeal to the adult. The Sunday School leaves nobody on the outside. An infant in a Sunday School ministry is affected and influenced by the atmosphere of a spiritual Sunday School. Someone has said that a child learns half of everything they will know by the time they are seven years of age. The Sunday School can reach them in these formative years.

I will discuss the importance of promotion later in this book. When we realize that boys and girls and adults can be reached; when we realize that the Sunday School makes it possible for us to reach them, we will have a great Sunday School.

(5) ***THE SUNDAY SCHOOL CAN SERVE THE ENTIRE FAMILY.*** An exciting Sunday School will attract families. The Sunday School will produce

social contacts. Going to Sunday School is something the entire family can do. There is a place for everybody and each member is wanted. Each person is needed. It affords the entire family a place to serve, a place to worship, a place to learn, a place to fellowship, and a social as well as a spiritual contact.

(6) ***THE SUNDAY SCHOOL IS THE GREATEST TEACHING FACILITY.*** Jesus is referred to as THE TEACHER. He was called TEACHER more than by any other title. He taught His disciples. He taught the multitudes. He commissioned the church to teach all the nations. (Matthew 28:19)

The work "TEACH" is used 109 times in the Bible. The word "TEACHES" is used fourteen times in the Scripture. Mark 6:34 and Mark 8:31 says that Jesus "began to teach them." (Matthew 28:29) Believers are commanded to teach all the nations. (Acts 4:18) The early disciples did teach in the name of Jesus. (Acts 5:42) The early church "ceased not to teach and preach." Teachers are placed in the church as "ministry gifts." (I Corinthians 12:28; Ephesians 4:11; Titus 2:3,4; and Hebrews 5:12)

(7) ***THE SUNDAY SCHOOL STABILIZES AND STRENGTHENS THE CHURCH.*** When people are involved in a church program, they are apt to stay closely affiliated with that church. It is important that people are given responsibility. We, too often, tell people that they must be busy in the Lord's work, and we challenge them to dedicate themselves to serving. However, we are often guilty of failing to place in their hands a **specific area of responsibility**. Christians will work if they are told what to do. Christians are faithful when they are instructed in

what is expected of them. The Sunday School provides this instruction.

(8) ***THE SUNDAY SCHOOL PLACES AN EMPHASIS ON CHRISTIAN CHARACTER AS WELL AS CHRISTIAN SERVICE.*** The Bible becomes the important feature in a Christ-centered Sunday School. The Word of God is the **TEXT BOOK**. There is no other ministry in the church that puts the Bible in as many hands and hearts and homes.

The emphasis and importance is placed on attendance, faithfulness to the church, and loyalty to the pastor. The Sunday School instructs people in prayer, Christian living, and Christ-centered fellowship.

(9) ***THE SUNDAY SCHOOL AFFORDS THE PERSONAL CONTACT WITH PEOPLE OUTSIDE THE CHURCH.*** A well-organized Sunday School is so structured that it makes it possible for contacts in the home. This is very important! It is possible to promote and to inspire people to contact their friends and their neighbors. The Sunday School also permits an effective visitation program. This places an emphasis on friendliness, personal concern, and spiritual well-being.

(10) ***THE SUNDAY SCHOOL PROVIDES A STRUCTURE ON WHICH THE ENTIRE CHURCH PROGRAM CAN BUILD.*** The church is BIG business. The work of the church is IMPORTANT BUSINESS!! It is eternal business! It is God's business!

Every church can build a great Sunday School. There is no such things as a Gospel-hardened community. We can blame the lost! We can believe that people will not come to church! We can declare that men love their sins! The church can insist that the outsider refuses to believe the Bible! We can preach that the masses have rejected Christ!

BUT, before we complete a catalog of reasons why people do not come to church, perhaps some honest examination might indicate that the reasons for their indifference may lie within the church. We must share the blame! We are guilty! God will hold us responsible!

We are urged by God's Word to go into the highways and byways and compel men and women to come in (Luke 14:23). Jesus implored His believers to pray that laborers would be thrust into the field. "The fields are white unto the harvest." Men are hungry for God! The masses can be reached! They must be reached! The Sunday School can reach them!

CHAPTER THREE

LEADERSHIP DETERMINES GROWTH

Jesus spent the three years of His earthly ministry training leaders. He understood well that His Church would not grow without properly trained and dedicated leadership.

The Apostle Paul was the great church builder of the New Testament. He gave his life to establishing churches and to the teaching and training of young men who could take the responsibility of leadership after the churches were established. Much effort and care was given in his instruction to Timothy and Titus and to many others, such as the elders in Ephesus. (See Acts 20.)

Without qualified leadership, the church will flounder. Without trained leadership, the church cannot grow and develop. Without spiritual leadership, the members of the local body will never develop their "giftings." It is safe to state that churches without strong leadership will not mature nor grow.

FIVE THINGS EVERY CHURCH LEADER MUST UNDERSTAND

(1) *A leader must be aware of fads and trends that affect the church.*

It is not only important to be AWARE of them, but a leader must BEWARE of them. Fads come and go. It is easy to become "taken up" with and involved in some new thing that will draw the attention of people for a season. These fads usually pass as quickly as they come. Over the past many years, we have seen the church influenced and affected by fads in worship, in music, in preaching styles, in church growth efforts, and in doctrines that are not sound or scriptural. To attempt to build a church without the fundamental basics is to build on sand. The fads will change and the work will suffer.

Then, there are trends...every leader must be keenly aware of the trends. There is a trend in our society toward both parents working outside the home. There is a trend to the single parent family. Today, we have to deal with the mobile society.

There is a "crunch" on the time that people have to give to the church and its ministry. There are trends now away from Sunday evening service. In some cases, a Saturday night service is taking the place of the Sunday morning service.

It is not always easy to recognize trends. It is also very difficult to know how we should respond to the trends. However, not to do so is to lose our effectiveness in reaching and winning people.

There are some very important trends that are taking place in American society that the church must recognize:

(a) There is a rapid and dramatic increase in the single-parent home.

(b) The population is a lot more mobile.

(c) There is a tendency in society not to be loyal to or committed to a local church and its programs. Many churchgoers today freely move from one congregation to another.

(d) There is a trend in some areas away from traditional services and traditional schedules for meetings.

(e) In the major cities, the inner city is being neglected, and people are moving to communities on the outskirts of the cities.

These are just a few of the many trends that seem apparent as the church struggles to minister to the people.

(2) *Leaders must struggle to maintain balance in the local church.*

This is perhaps the hardest thing that any pastor has to accomplish ... the balance between worship and the ministry of the Word, balance in challenging the people to reach the local community as well as to touch the "uttermost part of the earth." The balance between having many outside ministries and programs and developing local talent. The balance between having social programs and involvement in prayer meetings and Bible study. The list goes on and on.

How much traditional music should be used? How much contemporary music is to be allowed? What is the balance as it relates to dress code? What are the standards of holiness? What are the rules and regulations for membership in the local church? Is there a balance maintained in what is being taught and preached? Do we use the hymn book or choruses? Do we stand in worship for long periods of time? Do we carefully follow a program or do we move solely by inspiration? What are the disciplines?

All of these things (and much more) must be considered by every leader in the local church.

(3) ***The leader must love and enjoy preaching and teaching.***

People must be fed. The Word of God is the instrument that God uses to produce faith. Faith comes by hearing the Word!!

Preaching must be from the Bible. Preaching must be practical. The Word must be applied to the everyday needs of the people. If the people are not strongly established in the basic doctrines of the church, they will not be stable, loyal, and dependable.

Too often, so much time is given to other things in the service until little is left for teaching "the household of faith." Jesus is referred to as "Teacher" one hundred and nine times in the New Testament. The great commission instructs us to "go into all the world and teach." Leaders are to "disciple" believers. Disciples are learners. People cannot learn without a teacher.

(4) ***Every leader must know they are called of God and that they are in the will of God.***

The Apostle Paul was able to say "I, Paul, a servant of Jesus Christ, CALLED to be an apostle, separated unto the gospel of God." (Romans 1:1) He could state forthrightly that he was a CALLED servant. In I Corinthians 1:1, he repeats: "Paul, CALLED to be an apostle of Jesus Christ through the will of God, ..."

Paul knew he was ***CALLED*** and Paul knew that he was in the will of God. He further declares in Ephesians 1:1 ... "Paul, an apostle of Jesus Christ by the will of God, to the saints ...." He continues in chapter five by saying:

> ***"Wherefore, be ye not unwise, but understanding what the will of the Lord is."***
> ***Ephesians 5:17***

Too many preachers do not have the sense that they are in the will of God. Sometimes the CALL of God is in question in their minds. Until these two matters are settled, a person can never be the leader that God intends. Do you have the CALL of God on your life? Are you in the WILL of God in your ministry today?

(5) ***Leaders must refrain from referring to personal crisis in their ministry while passing through the crisis.***

There will be reverses. There will be dark and difficult times. It is a mistake to speak of these difficulties while you are passing through the valley. It is easy to get a distorted view of what is taking place. Under the pressure of the difficulty, there is danger that things will be said that will produce great harm.

It is easy to see things from a wrong perspective when you are fighting the battle. It is best to wait until you have passed through the difficulty. Then, you can reach back into the circumstance and draw sweetness out of a sour and difficult experience.

ADVICE TO LEADERSHIP

(1) *Make changes but make them slowly and carefully.*

Changes should not be made until much consideration has been given to the proposed change. Communication and transparency is vitally important. It is critical that the proposed change be shared with as many people as possible on a one-to-one basis.

Very few people are comfortable with change. Changes disturb our sense of security. Many times a change can cause people to feel that there is some ulterior motive in the change.

Changes MUST be made. There will not be growth or development without it. When there is no change, there is stagnation. Growth will be hindered. So, prepare well for the change. When you are successful with one change, it will be easier to make a second change. A new leader should move with extreme caution before making changes.

(2) *Avoid confrontation.*

It is very easy to polarize your congregation. Time, indeed, is a healer. When differences arise, give much time to prayer. Guard against snap decisions. Ask advice from those who have experience. Listen carefully to those who are involved in a problem. Quick confrontation usually results in division.

Recognize that there is some strong lay leader promoting the confrontation. If you antagonize this "real leader," those over whom he has influence will rally to him. Churches that run under one hundred are usually controlled by some lay person. The congregation looks to them before they respond to the preacher.

(3) *Give authority slowly.*

You can never retrieve it once it has been released. In the church, there is often the danger of appointing someone to an office or a position simply for the purpose of pleasing or influencing some individual. An office should never be created for a person. An office or a ministry should be established because there is a **need!!**

Then, the person who is qualified to minister can be given the position. There are men who have been designated Deacons who do not fill the office of a deacon. There are men who are serving as local church elders who do not fill the scriptural responsibilities or qualifications of an elder. Men and women have been placed on boards and given positions of authority in order to satisfy ego. Many times when this authority is placed upon them, they begin to usurp a power that was never intended.

(4) *Don't push your vision too fast.*

It is easy for leadership to get excited about some program, projects or expansion. The leader may be spending a great deal of time thinking about and planning some vision or program. It must be remembered that the people in the congregation have not been inspired. The church may not be aware of the need or the burden. They may see your burden as an impossible challenge. It may cause the person in the pew to become fearful that the church will be involved in something too big for the congregation. If the people sense that the pastor is not making a good decision, they may resist the program. They know that if things do not work well, the pastor can move to another church. Then, the local church is left to face the consequences of this poor decision. A pastor must go slowly when presenting his vision.

If the Lord has given you some direction, if He has called you to some special task, if you feel inspired to a particular accomplishment…take time to share it. Share it person-to-person. Share it in small groups. Talk to those that you know will agree with you and stand with you. Generate enthusiasm **BEFORE** you ask for a commitment. Call people to prayer.

Bring in someone from the outside who can support you in your vision. Be sure to make the plan very, very clear. Give the purpose and reason behind the challenge. Detail how it can be done and how it can be financed. Explain the potential and the results. In short, DON'T PUSH YOUR VISION TOO FAST!!

(5) *Leaders must refrain from getting too close to lay people.*

A pastor must realize that he is the leader to each person in the assembly. All must be treated with the same dignity and respect. Everyone must be given an equal place in his heart and in his life. When a leader fellowships more with one person than he does with others, there will be those in the congregation who will feel that they are rejected or unimportant.

It is a dangerous thing for a leader to go to a lay person with personal problems and difficulties. Counsel and help needs to come from someone else in the ministry or from some friend who is not a part of the local church. You will expose yourself to criticism and to accusations when you, as a leader, become too intimate with a member in the church. Many a pastor has been devastated because trust and confidence has been broken. In some cases, what was shared in a time of extreme difficulty was used as a weapon to destroy the pastor.

There is a certain professional manner that must be maintained by the *"CALLED"* person of God. The leader stands alone. This is why it is important for every pastor to be involved in some fellowship of ministers and churches. Leaders need contact with other leaders. There needs to be a place where you can share and where you can be helped by others who are experiencing difficulty.

It is important that ministers attend ministers' institutes and conferences. It gives the minister an opportunity to fellowship with others who are facing similar experiences. Friendship, closeness, and intimate sharing must be done on a peer level with others who are involved in the ministry.

(6) *A pastor needs to limit the time he gives to counseling.*

There are people that God has called into the counseling ministry. They are gifted counselors. However, there are many dangers associated with the ministry of counseling.

After more than 50 years in the ministry, I would advise ministers to be extremely cautious in the time they give to personal and private counseling sessions for the following reasons:

(a) Most people who seek counseling do not follow the advice that is given.

(b) Most people know what is right and wrong in their situation. They are looking for an excuse or some way to avoid the obvious decision.

(c) Others use the counselor to their own advantage. The counselor is misquoted. On occasions the counselee uses the advice the counselor gives for ulterior purposes.

(d) If people with deep spiritual needs would faithfully attend worship services and give time to seeking the Lord and the guidance of the Holy Spirit, there would be no need for a private counseling time. Most of the people who have sought my counseling over the years have not been faithfully involved in the ministry and vision of the church.

(e) Counseling demands a lot of time and drains much strength away from the minister.

(f) A minister can open himself up to so much negativism, criticism, and problems that his ministry is adversely affected.

The needs of the people will be met when the Word of God is prayerfully preached, when there is a fellowship among the believers that provides social contact and spiritual strength, and when there is allotted time for prayer and Bible study.

(7) *A pastor needs to have an office in the church building.*

It is important that office hours be established. People of the congregation and the community need to know that a pastor and his staff are available. When a minister does not maintain office hours, it is easy for people to trespass into the home life and schedule of the parsonage.

The pastor's home is not an extension of the church's ministry. When the pastor is available, because of consistent hours in the office, people will know that the minister is accessible. It is easy for the pastor's home to become an office and a study. This puts undue burden on the minister's spouse and family. The business community needs to know that the pastor is a professional.

(8) *It is important that the minister make friends of community leaders.*

Most pastors are so involved in the local church fellowship that they are insulated and isolated from what is happening outside the church. A pastor needs to acquaint himself with the mayor, the chief of police, the sheriff, the newspaper editor, a doctor, a lawyer, the president of the bank, the superintendent of schools, the chaplain at the hospital or prison, and business leaders in general. The more credibility that the minister has in the community the more effective his work will be. You will soon discover that people in the business community appreciate your interest, your prayers, and your willingness to be available. The leader who has taken the time to develop these kinds of contacts can make void any negative words about the church that may be passed around in the community.

(9) *Leadership must be extremely cautious in financial matters.*

When bills are not paid on time, we lose our witnessing power. Credibility and accountability is important in money matters. An audited report is important. Clear communication concerning money policies is necessary. A church will not grow if questions concerning finances persist.

(10) *If someone in the congregation indicates that they are going to leave the fellowship, it is important that you do not attempt to persuade them to remain in the fellowship.*

Once a person becomes dissatisfied to the point of severing relationship with the church, it is best that you send them on their way and commit them to the hand of God. In most cases, when people are persuaded not to leave, they remain in the church and spread dissatisfaction in the local body. The church will be strong when each member knows that they are in the will of God attending the local church.

(11) *It is wise for a minister to take the following precautions:*

(a) Do not make visitation calls alone. If your wife cannot accompany you, be sure some associate does.

(b) Remove all locks from the pastor's office door. Let staff people know that you have an open-door policy.

(c) Do not counsel members of the opposite sex without your spouse being present.

(d) Guard against flattery and be aware that your ego and pride can destroy you.

(e) Always speak positively concerning your spouse and give open expressions of your love and respect for her and the members of your family.

(f) Be extremely cautious about sharing personal problems with anyone in your local church body.

(g) Take your wife with you everyplace that it is possible to do so.

(h) Refuse to get into a vehicle with a member of the opposite sex and avoid being in a church building alone with a member of the opposite sex.

(12) *A minister is susceptible to failure and weakness when weary or under great stress.*

Take time to recuperate. There must be occasions when the minister and his family can get away from the demands of the ministry. Not to do so is to expose yourself to many problems.

(13) *Develop a personal visitation program.*

Carry an index card of a person who needs to be visited. Give that card to a member of the church or a staff person who can relate to the person who needs to be visited. Ask them to call in the home at their very earliest convenience. Be sure they inform the person visited that they were sent there at the request of the pastor. Give the person who is making the call a little gift to give to the person visited. When a minister will carry a list of such cards with him, he can involve a lot of people in the visitation ministry.

(14) *Take a close look at the church facilities.*

Is the auditorium properly lit? Do the facilities need to be redecorated or landscaped? Is everything attractive and in order? A building that is not light, clean, and inviting will repulse people.

(15) *Set realistic goals.*

When a goal that has been set is reached, it brings great encouragement to the people. Don't set goals too high. An unreached goal can be disappointing and sometimes produces discouragement. Goals for attendance, finances, and other accomplishments must be challenging but reasonable.

(16) ***Give instructions and communicate with staff members and leaders in writing.***

So much is left undone or improperly done because communication was not clear.

THE RESPONSIBILITY OF LEADERSHIP

No person can assume the role of leadership in the "body of Christ" without carefully assessing what is expected of him. God's Word makes some clear-cut demands of leadership. A leader must be approved by the "body" and show evidence that the Holy Spirit has sanctioned his appointment. Leaders must show signs of true spirituality. The Bible is very clear in providing guidelines so we can judge if a person is indeed a "spiritual person!" Listed below are eight Scriptural references:

(1) A leader must have a willingness to restore a fallen or weak brother (Galatians 6:1). A leader must have a heart for the person who is hurt. A leader must reach out to someone who has stumbled, fallen, or has been overtaken in a fault.

(2) A leader must show that he understands spiritual truths (I Corinthians 2:11-12).

(3) A SPIRITUAL PERSON avoids contention, strife, divisions, and arguments (I Corinthians 3:1-3). There are always divisive issues raised in a "body of believers." It is impossible to keep these divisive issues from flowing through the "body." A leader refuses to get involved in such contentions and strife. This is the important mark of a true spiritual leader.

(4) A leader has a positive awareness of the will of God (I Corinthians 2;15-16; Ephesians 5:16-19).

(5) A leader is patient toward the weak and does everything to edify his fellow believer (Romans 15:1-3). (Read very carefully the entire 14th chapter. Note particularly verse 10.)

(6) A SPIRITUAL PERSON is aware of the "spirituals" listed in I Corinthians 12:4-11 and is willing to seek God that these "gifts" will function in the local "body." He is also capable of "judging" whether or not these manifestations are indeed spiritual and functioning properly (I Corinthians 12:1; 14:29 and 14:37).

(7) A SPIRITUAL PERSON offers spiritual sacrifices and enters into spiritual worship. He is not given to the things of this world. He is more consumed with worship, praise and blessing God than with the pleasures and appetites of the world system (I Peter 2:5; Ephesians 5:19).

(8) A SPIRITUAL PERSON possesses a spiritual mind (Romans 8:6) and therefore does not give place to carnal things. Unclean thoughts, unclean stories, careless and foolish words and silly jesting are opposed to the character of the Holy Spirit. Philippians 2:5-8 is a beautiful example of a spiritual mind.

The above list suggests a few characteristics of a *SPIRITUAL PERSON.* Leaders must manifest these qualities. This is the criteria placed before us by the Scriptures.

The Holy Spirit will raise up such leaders when we seek the Lord for the development of leadership in His "body."

Leadership determines what will happen in the local congregation. If a leader does not follow certain practices and principles, there will be no increase. Where there is a strong church, you will find a capable leader. *LEADERSHIP DOES DETERMINE GROWTH!!!*

CHAPTER FOUR

THE MINISTER AND HIS OFFICE

There are certain guidelines that must be followed if a minister is to be effective in the church. When these guidelines are followed, the minister becomes effective and the church becomes strong.

(1) An adequate office must be established in the church.

(2) The minister needs to dress the way other professional people dress in the community. How does the doctor dress? How does the principal of the school dress? How does the president of the bank dress? A minister needs to look like a professional.

(3) Every office needs an adequate telephone system. As the church grows the minister needs a private line so that his family can get through to him when necessary.

(4) A growing church should use a post office box number. Limit mail that would be sent to your home.

(5) Obtain the services of a good secretary as quickly as possible. When a church starts, volunteer help can be of tremendous benefit.

(6) Establish regular office hours.

(7) There are many people in the church who are willing to assist as volunteers for stuffing mail, helping with the bulletin, preparing bulletin boards, answering the telephone, and many other job responsibilities.

(8) Provide good stationery.

(9) Set up an adequate record system for church members, attendance keeping, financial records, etc.

(10) Build a usable file system for correspondence and subject material for the minister.

(11) Use two signatures on all checks.

(12) Return telephone calls immediately.

(13) Answer your mail. Ministers are some of the worst transgressors. Over the years I have seen ministers who were so careless in replying to their mail. Many wait until the very last minute before they will respond to a registration in a fellowship conference. Others will let mail set on their desks for weeks when an evangelist or missionary is desperate for some response. Others will cancel meetings at the last moment because they have neglected their mail.

(14) Every minister should carefully schedule his time. Each hour of the day needs to be scheduled, each day of the week, each week of the month.

(15) Buy good equipment. It will be used for a long time and needs to be the best that is available.

(16) A minister should refrain from counting offerings or banking the money.

(17) Set a dress code for staff members.

(18) Prepare a handbook for employees. Every detail concerning employee-employer relationship should be clearly described. Things such as pay, raises, vacations, sick days, days off, and job descriptions should be in writing.

A church will not grow unless a well organized office is established. The office and its staff is the heart of the entire ministry. When it is strong, the church will grow.

CHAPTER FIVE

SUNDAY SCHOOL PLATEAUS

HERE IS THE KEY.... This chapter could give you the answer. If your church is not growing, then read this chapter very, very carefully. According to a recent survey, it was determined that eighty-six percent of the churches in America have reached a point of stagnation. There is no growth. Churches reach plateaus. If careful consideration is not given to this situation, the church will not only level out in its attendance but will begin to decrease.

Much of church growth can be contributed to transfer of members from one church to another. People who become dissatisfied because a church is not growing can be drawn to a church that is alive and increasing. Recent statistics have proven that over ninety percent of the churches who are growing are doing so at the expense of the church that is not growing.

THE FIRST PLATEAU

THE FIRST PLATEAU CAN BE IDENTIFIED AS A CONGREGATION WITH **100 OR LESS PEOPLE** IN ATTENDANCE. This church has many characteristics. It most likely has become a "family affair." The members can be blood relatives, or they can be such a closely related people that the church has become a clique.

The church that is running around 100 in attendance and has not grown over a period of several months begins to isolate and insulate itself from the "outsider." A church of this size is often very difficult for a visitor or newcomer to be comfortable attending. They are made to feel that they are not a part.

A church can remain at 100 or less for many, many reasons:

(1) A great emphasis is placed on social activity and family relationships in the small group. Members feel that if the church should grow they would lose their intimacy.

(2) Sometimes people feel threatened when an effort is made to reach out and touch others. Their position in the church may be in jeopardy.

(3) Members of a small church can feel that leadership will not afford them the same amount of attention if there is an increase in the church.

(4) There is no plan or effort to reach new people.

(5) The group tends to become so informal that care is not given to good manners, discipline, and dignified worship habits.

There are many, many characteristics that identify the church that has reached this first plateau. Some very important changes must be met if a church is going to grow to the second plateau. When these changes are carefully considered and implemented, the church can break away from this first plateau and start growing. Here are some of these changes:

(1) Schedule the activity of the Sunday School hour. The attention span for a child in the first to the fourth grade is between six and eight minutes. This means that a one-hour Bible School class must have at least eight to twelve different activities that will be taking place in order to hold the attention of a boy or girl. **(Refer to Chapter 6.)**

(2) Classes must be structured to follow the grade levels of the elementary school in your community. Plans must be made for a first grade class, a second grade class, third grade class, etc.

(3) The classroom needs to be as much like the elementary schoolroom as possible.

(4) A strict schedule must be followed for all departments. Classes must begin on time and close on time. It is necessary to create a classroom atmosphere. Children are accustomed to the school classroom. The church must duplicate this condition.

(5) **Goals must be set** for attendance and offerings.

(6) It must be remembered that "sheep produce sheep." Shepherds do not produce sheep! Every child has a playmate, a neighbor, or a friend. Children need to be inspired to bring their peers to the Bible class.

(7) **Plans must be made** to put classes under department heads. There must be a nursery depart-

ment, a beginners department, a junior department, a junior high department, etc. These structural plans need to be carefully presented to the people.

(8) Room must be available for growth and increase.

(9) The pastor of the small church must lead the way in inviting new people into the assembly.

(10) People must be taught and trained to greet and accept the first timer and the newcomer.

(11) A follow-up program must be instituted so that every newcomer is contacted.

(12) Services must run on a careful schedule. If church services run overtime, new people will not continue to respond.

The church that runs under 100 in attendance must be prepared to make dramatic changes if the Sunday School is to move above this first plateau. **A church must overcome a RESISTANCE TO CHANGE.** Most people are deeply concerned and have difficulty accepting new ways , new programs, new plans, and new methods. Some will respond to change with criticism. Others will remain silent and uncooperative. Still others will "quit the program."

Resistance to change is caused when we do not carefully lay plans for the change. I want to make some suggestions to help overcome this resistance.

(1) ***Invite people to be a part in all decision making.*** When people can be involved and have an opportunity to see all sides of an issue and all of the implications, it is easier for them to accept change. Leaders have a great responsibility for them to accept change. Leaders have to educate individuals so that

they can react to a proposed change. We must create an atmosphere where teachers and workers will feel that they are a part of all the decision making.

(2) ***Create an atmosphere that encourages workers to experiment with something new.*** We must be sure that we do not condemn the old. It is important that we focus on the positive by providing the necessary current materials and the opportunity for change. A training program is required so that each worker knows how to make a change. Someone has to work closely with the teachers so no one is allowed to "get discouraged."

(3) ***Provide a program of continuous explanation so that you are keeping abreast of everything new that has been offered.*** Take advantage of conventions, urge your key workers to visit in successful Sunday Schools. See what the other person is doing. If teachers are continuously exposed to changing ideas outside their circle, they are not so frustrated when a change comes home.

(4) ***A leader must be willing to be open.*** A leader must encourage workers to try something new in the class. Be slow to criticize any effort being made.

When a leader is willing to accept sincerely the worries, complaints, and suggestions; he promotes acceptance of his own ideas.

(5) ***Be aware of personality traits.*** Some people are naturally reticent. Change is difficult for them. We must know how a change is going to affect a person and their relationship with others. People need to be encouraged and bolstered so they have a sense of worth. Each one must feel they are a part of

the change. Everything must be done to eliminate the feeling of insecurity.

(6) ***Don't move too fast.*** Changes only work when people will cooperate. We must move slowly and carefully. If we do, changes can be made effectively.

(7) ***Be sure you are prepared and be convinced that the change is necessary.*** If you make a change and you have made a mistake, it will be more difficult to institute a change the next time.

We must carefully determine every **plan of action.** Do everything to gain the cooperation and the support of your workers. Of course, we need the Holy Spirit to guide us "through" every change that is made.

There are always tensions when a change is made. This cannot be avoided. However, we can minimize these tensions if we are prepared in every detail.

The teachers must be assured that they can handle the change. You can give them this confidence.

DISCOURAGEMENT hinders growth. But God said to Joshua, "Be thou strong and very courageous..." God was saying, "Don't be discouraged." Discouragement is a contagion. It is a spiritual disease that will paralyze. ***When discouragement strikes — death sets in, growth is hampered, and the Sunday School falters and fails.*** Here are some suggestions to fight this enemy:

(1) Never count your losses! Minimize the negative!

(2) Always testify to the good, the growth, the accomplishments.

(3) Be careful that two negative people are not permitted to work together.

(4) Prepare your plans carefully. Be sure that you avoid errors. When we miscalculate, we open the door to defeat.

(5) Set goals that can be attained! Increase your goals in steps so that your workers and staff can rejoice in victory!

(6) Be sure people are not bored with responsibility. If there is no challenge, if workers cannot see some evidence of success, they will grow weary. Help the area that tends to fail or "let down."

(7) Promote people to a new assignment! Sometimes a person is uncomfortable where they are. Often there are personality clashes. The environment may be depressing. You may have someone working in a department that does not feel comfortable in this position. There is a place for everyone! There is a spot where a key person can function and be happy and successful. It is the task of the leader to place that person in the right "spot." This will do more to curb discouragement than anything else.

(8) **Discouragement is a spirit!!** It is Satan's trick (device). A wise administrator will prepare people for an attack. Spend time with your workers! Call them in for prayer. They need to know that they are in a conflict. (Ephesians 6:10-12) *A word from you as a leader can help them in the heat of the battle.*

(9) Every person must feel they are a part. Leaders can make workers know that their job is necessary. Tell them your goals and your aims. Share with your

workers your burdens. We must involve each one spiritually and emotionally.

(10) Be alert to discouragement. Leaders must he quick to realize that this enemy can destroy. God has promised to lift a standard against our enemies.

Church growth is hindered because of resistance to change, discouragement, and LACK OF DISCIPLINE.

(1) God's people are undisciplined as it relates to promptness and "being on time." Ministers and leaders are often to blame. Every activity should begin precisely on time. There must never be a moment's delay!!

All of us know that promptness is demanded at work, at school, and in very other area of life. Television programs run on schedule. Airlines and transportation systems strive to be prompt. Business men must make and meet appointments, but too often we let God's work run without discipline or dedication.

We have weak excuses for starting late or for arriving late. It is no wonder the "outsider" is not convinced that we are sincere, earnest, and dedicated. When God's people will be as dedicated as the "children of disobedience," we will witness a great success in the work of the ministry!

(2) Many "laborers for God" are **_not prepared._** This is a lack of discipline. It is difficult to challenge some to attend and participate in classes, seminars, and monthly meetings so that we can learn new methods, new techniques, and new approaches. Some are expecting God to do what God commanded us to do! We are commanded to "study to show thyself

approved unto God a workman that needeth not to be ashamed." God's work needs prepared vessels.

It is sad to permit teachers to go to the class without _**proper preparation**_. Leaders must be patient and diligent to teach workers how to communicate. Teachers need instructions in visual aids, scheduling, outline making, etc. An unprepared worker is not only undisciplined, but is also failing!

(3) **There is a thrill in working for God!!** We can lose our enthusiasm. The work can become dull and unexciting, if we are not aware and awake. When we relax, we lose our effectiveness. It takes effort, dedication, faith, and discipline to be enthusiastic. It is easy to murmur, to criticize, to be negative. God needs enthusiasts.

All through the Word we are admonished to "rejoice," to "tell all His wondrous works," to "offer a sacrifice of praise." Our enthusiasm will create growth and praises.

THE SECOND PLATEAU

Once a church begins to grow, if important organizational changes are made, the Sunday School (School of the Bible) can reach the second plateau. This plateau is around the 250 attendance mark. If changes are not made, once again growth will be hindered. Here are some suggestions.

(1) _**Departments must be graded**_ exactly as the school system. Never ask a child how old he is; ask him what grade he is in school.

(2) ***Departments must now be <u>divided into</u> <u>units.</u>*** Each unit must be under the direction of some staff personality. This demands a full-time worker. When one unit head can be placed to be responsible for two or three departments, these departments will then grow. (**Note Flow Charts in Chapter 6.**)

(3) ***These <u>unit heads</u> must be <u>responsible for</u> <u>visitation, promotion, and teacher training.</u>*** Most Sunday Schools that run five hundred to two thousand are forced to hire full-time workers. A department with 75 pupils will ordinarily minister to at least one hundred families. This involves more work than the average church running one hundred in Sunday School. This cannot be accomplished with volunteer labor. Now the church is big business!

(4) ***<u>A central office system</u>*** for all records must be carefully established. Without such planning and organizational proceedings, the church cannot grow. This is a difficult plateau to pass.

(5) ***<u>Every worker in your Sunday School must</u> <u>be assigned a specific work schedule.</u>*** This needs to be done in writing. When a Sunday School is running three or four hundred, it is difficult to keep the communication lines open. Most Christians want to work and serve God. They simply do not know what is expected of them. Work assignments are absolutely essential. (**Refer to Chapter 6.**)

(6) ***<u>Insist on a strict schedule</u>*** in every class. The schedules should allow for a <u>change every eight to twelve minutes.</u> There is nothing any more important to a successful Sunday School class than adhering to a strict schedule of events. (**Refer to Chapter 6.**)

(7) ***Demand teacher discipline.*** Teachers must be <u>on time.</u> Teachers must <u>be prepared.</u> Teachers must <u>never read their material to the class.</u> Teachers must <u>be flexible and pliable.</u> Teachers must <u>be cooperative.</u> Teachers must <u>care enough to visit</u> members of their class. Teachers must <u>plan for social activities</u> for their students. Without this discipline, there will not be a successful Sunday School class. Without successful classes, there is no successful Sunday School. **(Refer to Chapter 6.)**

(8) ***Remember that sheep produce sheep.*** No one can reach a first-grader better than another first-grader. Promotion is necessary. <u>Reward</u> your students for their ministry. <u>Challenge them to bring others.</u>

In the following pages I have inserted some suggested **FLOW CHARTS** to give some guidelines for organizational structuring and planning. The church with an attendance of around 100 is similar to a family owned neighborhood business. When the church grows to 250 or over, the church is then compared to a corporation. It is time to structure independent and self-supporting departments. It is time to build a strong staff. It is time to think about the training of department heads.

There are four very important characteristics in a growing Sunday School. There must be ***COMMUNICATION, COMPETITION, CONSECRATION, and CHANGE.***

Let's look at ***COMMUNICATION.*** The best place to start is with the pastor. It is important that the pastor sit down and share carefully his vision and burden with key people. The pastor needs to lay out a plan, a program, a road map. Be very sure that these key people thoroughly understand the direction to go.

I will suggest that your plan be written. Give instructions to your workers in a written form.

It is extremely important that regular meetings with staff workers be conducted. Use your chalk-board. Prepare a questionnaire. Open the session to questions and answers. Prepare charts and graphs. The more you communicate, the more effective the work will be. **It takes time to be successful.**

A Sunday School will grow if a mailing list is prepared and used. A mailing list can be developed according to zones of a community, zip code numbers, according to school districts, or according to grades. Many growing churches use a combination of the above groupings for their list. The business world knows the importance of advertising. If a product is going to be sold, people must be educated. **A good mailing list is a must!!**

There is nothing any more important than meeting with small groups to discuss the church program. Meet with the secretaries separately. Meet with the teachers often. Give clear direction to department heads. Be available to the transportation personnel. Jesus knew the importance of preaching, relating, communicating. We were commanded to propagate. **A Sunday School will grow if we keep the lines of communication open!**

Let's look at *COMPETITION*. This is the name of the game in our society. Our children compete at school. They compete in sports; they compete in their social life. Society has learned the benefits of competition. There is competition in business, in school, and in play.

There needs to be goals and contests, incentives and rewards in the work of the Lord.

We are told that we will receive a reward when the Lord comes. **Jesus will reward us for faithful service.**

Encourage one class to do better than the other class. Encourage bus drivers to compete against another bus driver. Reward the winner, and encourage the loser.

Encourage the pupils to compete against the others in faithfulness to church, in bringing their friends to their class, and in participating in the activities. Competition creates enthusiasm. **Competition will make your Sunday School grow!**

A Sunday School will not grow without the *CONSECRATION* of its workers. Teachers and workers need to be graded and disciplined. Do they arrive on time? Are they prepared? Do they follow the plan? Your School will grow when its workers will dedicate themselves.

Support them in prayer. Share their burdens. Talk over your motives. Present a plan. **Challenge the people to be involved!**

Every growing Sunday School will *CHANGE.* It will be necessary to change teachers; to adjust to growth patterns. Teachers and workers must be willing to change from one classroom to another. Bus routes will change. The format of the class must change. When people refuse to change, the Sunday School refuses to grow.

I suggest that you beware of the following:

(1) Beware of assigning a teacher to a specific classroom so that they can become possessive of that particular classroom.

(2) Take great caution in permitting a teacher to raise money in their class to purchase things for their room. You may have to change them. Permitting them to buy their own equipment for a special room makes a change nearly impossible.

(3) Don't let the class follow the same format month after month! Insist on changes and alterations. Rearrange the class schedule. Alter the room and redecorate - make changes often.

Your Sunday School can grow!!

The Lord promises that laborers will be supplied if we will pray. Here are some suggestions for obtaining workers:

(1) ***Make your selection for workers very carefully and then spend time with this person.*** (Matthew 9:9, Matthew 10:1-14) Be sure this person understands exactly what is expected of him. Instill into him a burden for the work. Make the proposed worker feel the importance of his job. If he feels the need, he will respond.

(2) ***Workers are available if we will train.***

"Then came he to Derbe and Lystra: and behold, a certain disciple was there, named Timotheus, the son of a certain woman, which was a Jewess, and believed; but his father was a Greek: Which was well reported of by the brethren that were at Lystra and Iconium, Him would Paul

have to go forth with him; and took and circumcised him because of the Jews which were in those quarters: for they knew all that his father was a Greek. And as they went through the cities, they delivered them the decrees for to keep, that were ordained of the apostles and elders which were at Jerusalem. And so were the churches established in the faith, and increased in number daily."

Acts 16:1-5

I suggest that you invite an interested person to go into a department as a helper. Let them learn in the classroom. I would also suggest that the husband and wife be invited to work together in a department. This plan has been very successful.

Many people are willing to work if they know exactly what is expected of them.

(3) ***Establish a training class.*** (Luke 10:1-12) Jesus was the Great Teacher. He spent His life training others. He sat often with His pupils. There are several plans that can be followed:

(a) A class can be created for a course during the Sunday School hour.

(b) A training class can be established one night out of every month.

(c) Every new worker can be assigned to an experienced worker. It becomes the responsibility of the experienced worker to share and train.

(d) If the Sunday School classes are kept on careful schedule, a new worker can be assigned a brief period during the class schedule. This will help the new worker to relate to the class. This will build confidence.

(4) Our text suggests that we can ***pray for workers.*** The challenge and burden needs to be given to the people. If the leader will share the need, the people will respond. Call for special prayer meetings. The "Lord of the harvest" will call laborers.

(5) If there is a ***great deal of enthusiasm and success,*** there will be workers available. People want to be a part of a going church. We all love the excitement of accomplishment. There must never be any place for the negative. The emphasis must be on joy, pleasure, and victory.

FOUR THINGS EVERY TEACHER MUST KNOW

It is important that every teacher know the following things:

I. ***A teacher must know the student.***

(A) Background
(B) Environment Condition
(C) Spiritual Condition
(D) Comprehension Ability
(E) Interest Level
(F) Personality Problem
(G) Family Problem

Let me list some ways that a teacher can learn about his student:

(1) There are books available written about each age level. Visit the bookstore. Get in touch with the publishing house who furnished your church school material. **(Refer to Chapter 6.)**

(2) Visit regularly in the home. Make it brief, but visit!

(3) Acquaint yourself with the student. Call them by name.

(4) Pray specifically for them.

II. ***A teacher must know himself.*** Before a teacher goes to a class, the following questions must be considered:

    (A) Am I tired and irritable?
    (B) Am I discouraged?
    (C) Am I prepared? Am I really prepared?
    (D) Am I enthusiastic?
    (E) Am I friendly?
    (F) Have I prayed about this class?
    (G) Are there conditions and stresses in my own life and in my home or in the class?
    (H) Can I overlook problems?
    (I) Do I really believe in what I am doing today?
    (J) Do I have a positive attitude?

If we can answer these questions positively, we will be good teachers.

III. ___A teacher must know the lesson___. Let me list some important suggestions:

       (A) Start preparing ahead.
       (B) <u>NEVER</u> read your lesson to the class.
       (C) Always teach from an open Bible.
       (D) Follow a simple outline. Present specific thoughts.
       (E) Use visual aids. This is absolutely necessary.
       (F) Use illustrations.
       (G) Ask questions.
       (H) Leave the class wanting more.
       (I) Be sure that the lesson relates to the pupil.
       We must do more than give out facts. The lesson must relate.

IV. ___A teacher must know the entire church program___. A teacher is a part of the total. Here are some important suggestions:

       (A) Share the promotion of special days and special programs.
       (B) Be faithful to the whole church program.
       Attend the other services.
       (C) Stay in your class even when others are ministering. Your presence is meaningful and helpful.
       (D) Share the goals of the Sunday School.
       (E) Make church announcements in your class.

Once the Sunday School has reached 500 in attendance it has become "big business." Department heads must be full-time workers. Each department must be self-contained and properly staffed. There are several important considerations if the church is to continue its increase.

(1) The communication with staff must be clear and specific.

(2) Every grade must be assigned 52 lessons. (A lesson for each Sunday of the year.) These lessons must not change. A first-grade teacher must always teach the same 52 lessons. This must be followed through every grade level. If literature is changed every year, the cost for a growing School will become prohibitive.

(3) A proper schedule for each grade level must be set forth.

(4) There must be weekly contacts with workers such as teachers, department heads, secretaries, musicians, etc. This is best done through some kind of a weekly bulletin.

(5) There must be adequate facilities so the School can grow.

(6) Children's classes should never reach higher then 25-30 in a classroom.

(7) Social activities must be planned on a regular basis for students.

(8) There must be a promotional program that will encourage newcomers every quarter of the year.

(9) There must be teacher and worker training arrangements.

(10) The flow chart of responsibility must be clearly understood by every worker.

(11) There needs to be a handbook which gives the requirements for teachers and workers. This handbook must also spell out what the responsibilities for each worker are. An emphasis must be placed on soul winning and aggressive evangelism.

(12) Emphasis must be placed on the teaching of Biblical principles. Spiritual needs must be met.

(13) There must be an intense caring attitude among the workers.

(14) There must be a strong emphasis on loyalty, commitment, and discipleship.

(15) Goals and aims must be clearly stated.

(16) Workers must be recruited who are faithful to the entire church program and who respect the pastor as a God-given leader to the church.

If the church has reached a plateau, it is time to carefully analyze the situation. Changes must be made. It is my hope that the materials found in this book will provide guidelines for proper changes for the building of a strong and expanding foundation and for the increase in the effectiveness of the local church.

CHAPTER SIX

ORGANIZING FOR GROWTH

A growing church has a powerful influence in the community. When a church is weak, its impact is very small. The first church was a great church. The Holy Spirit placed three thousand members in it, and the entire city was affected by it. The growth of the early church impacted Jerusalem. God wants our churches to grow so that the community about us will be affected.

A church that is growing will be able to provide the kind of preaching and teaching that will strengthen its members. A church must be numerically, financially, and spiritually strong in order to reach outside its four walls.

There are many things that help contribute to the growing church. A growing church can provide a strong Christian educational program. A growing church can have a powerful ministry of music, singing, worship, choirs, and orchestras; and many other talents are available.

When a church begins to grow, it has great ability to reach out beyond its community and to touch other areas of the world. A growing church can be a missionary church.

A growing church can have youth ministry, children's programs, senior citizens outreach, and such ministries as singles ministry, unwed mothers, divorce problems, and many, many other outreaches. God wants the church to grow. The church is to be a **"spiritual hospital."** The church is to be a workshop…a place of worship…a place to serve…a house of fellowship…a tool to reach every member of every family in the community.

If the church is to grow, the leadership must show the members exactly what they are to do. Specific work detail must be provided. People want to be involved when they know what to do.

The church must reach new people. There must he new contacts. If we are not touching the outsider, the church cannot grow.

Leadership must provide a plan. What can be done to touch friends, relatives, neighbors, and the outsider?

DANGERS TO AVOID

1. Every care must be taken to see that spiritual things do not become common place.

2. Every worker must be made very sensitive to the dangers of becoming judgmental or legalistic.

3. An emphasis must always be placed upon the "work of the ministry." Ministry is labor. It is hard work.

4. Leadership must be encouraged to be faithful in prayers, in attendance, in life style, and in their tithes and offerings.

5. There must be enthusiasm among the workers toward the program that is presented to the church. It only takes one negative voice to create confusion, discouragement, and division.

6. Loyalty must be a prerequisite to ministry. Two cannot walk or work together unless they are in agreement. The New Testament church was powerful because they were in one accord. There is great power in unity.

7. Every care must be given to **avoid a critical attitude.**

8. It is possible to be so involved in labor, work and responsibility that a worker neglects their own spiritual and devotional life. It is possible to backslide while working for the kingdom of God.

9. Care must be given to see that a dedicated person is not overworked in the church. This will cause burnout, discouragement, and difficulty.

10. Time must be given for public recognition of those who are faithful in their ministry.

11. Celebrate each victory; minimize problems as much as possible.

12. Give much time to prayer and thanksgiving as the work of the Lord is blessed.

PRACTICAL HELPS FOR CHURCH STRUCTURE

In the following pages I want to share with you practical information concerning the structure of a church. The following pages contain sample flow charts. This will help in the organizing of a local church.

School of the Bible Flowchart

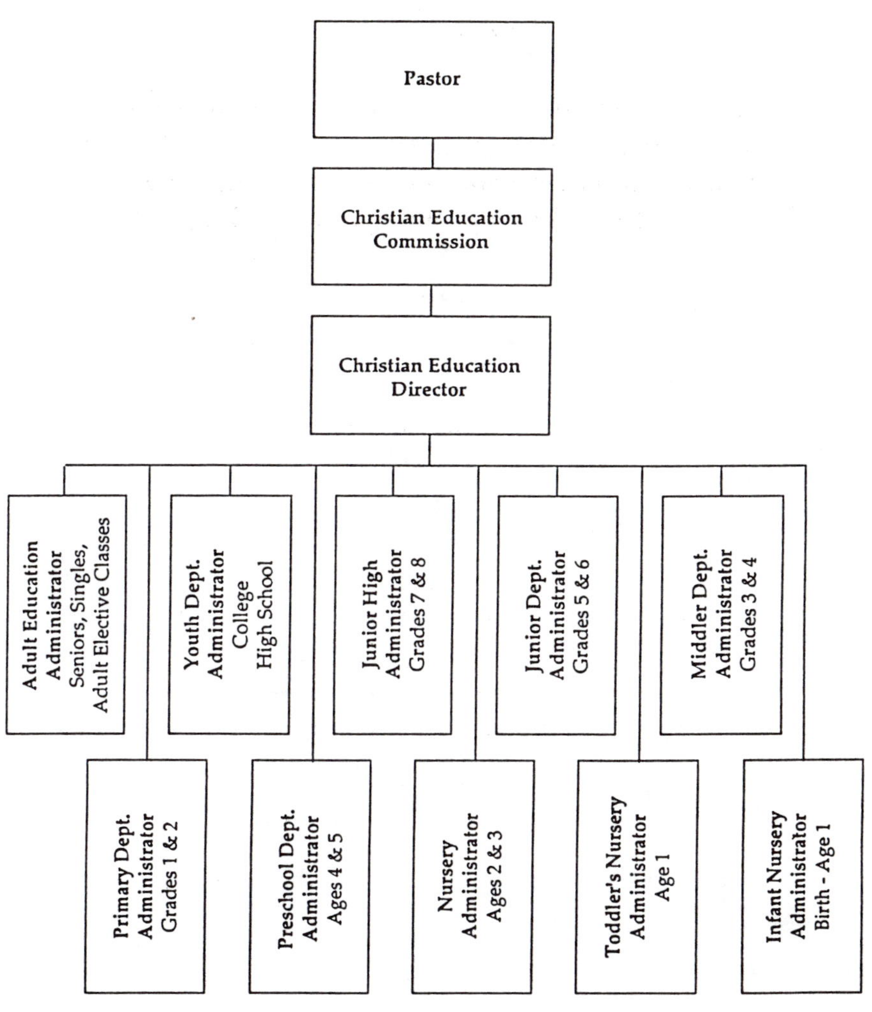

Adult Education Department Flowchart

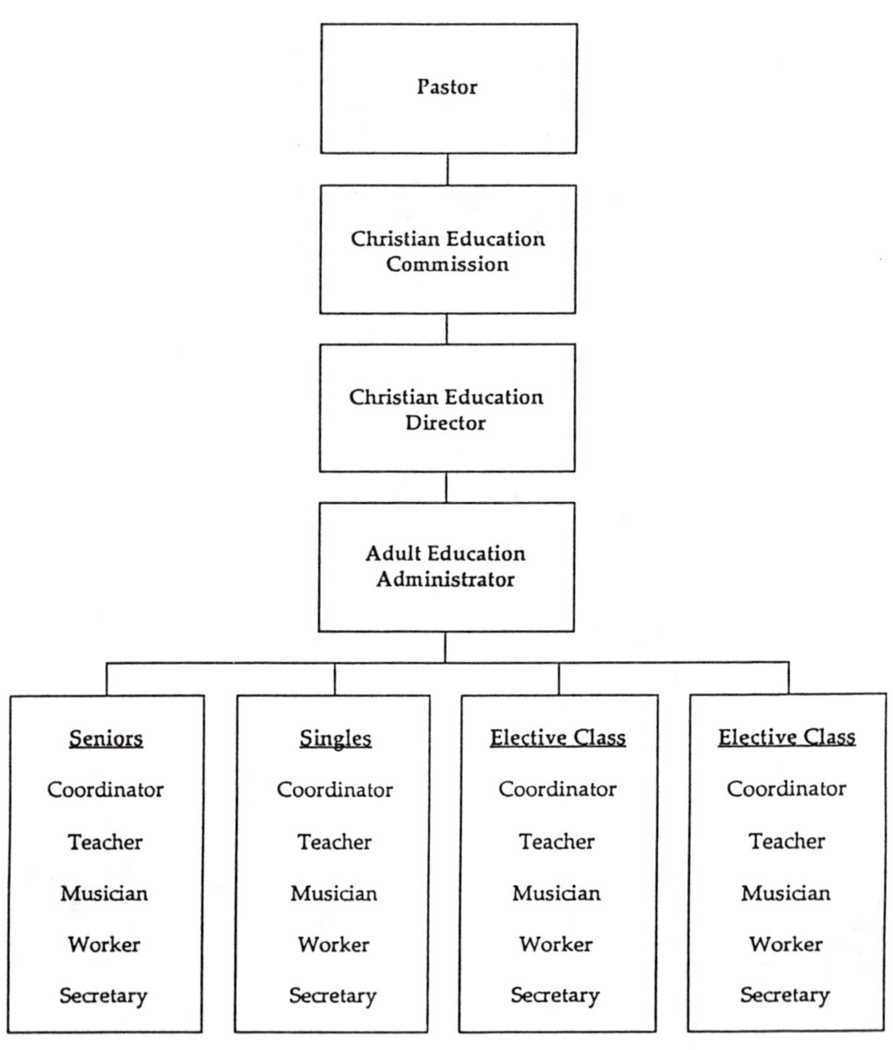

Crosswind Flowchart (Youth Department)

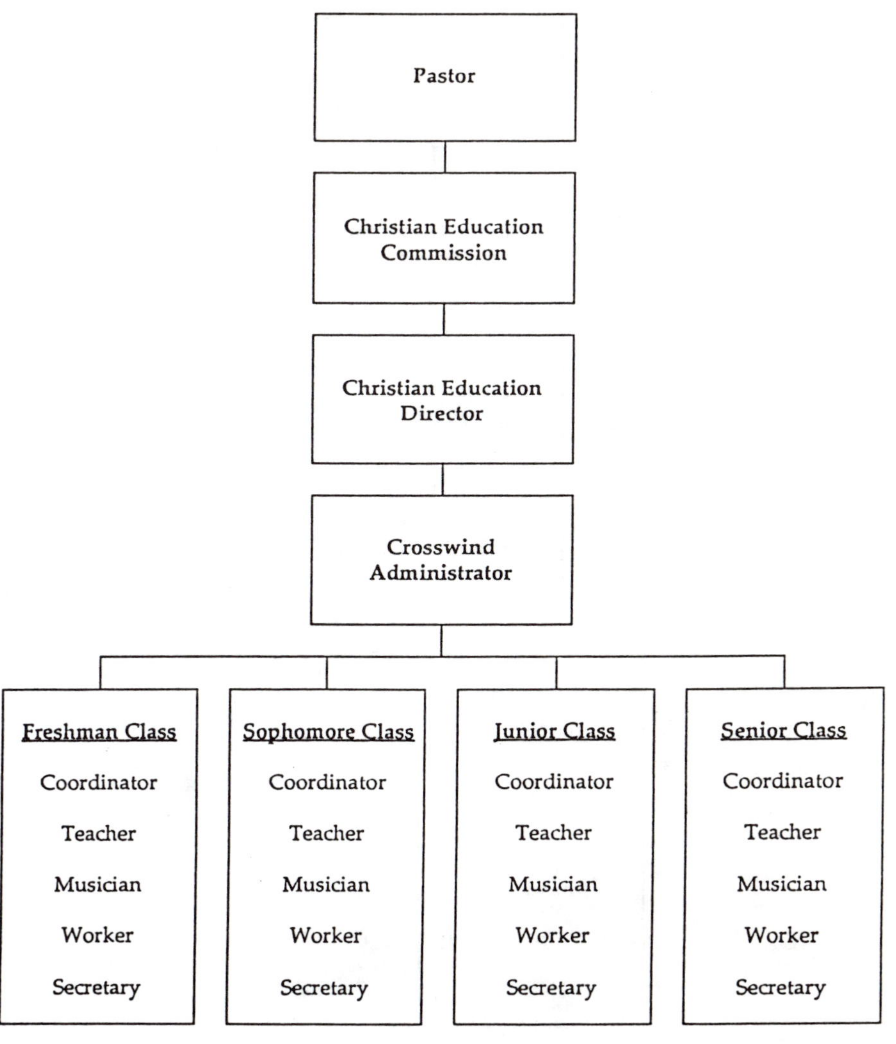

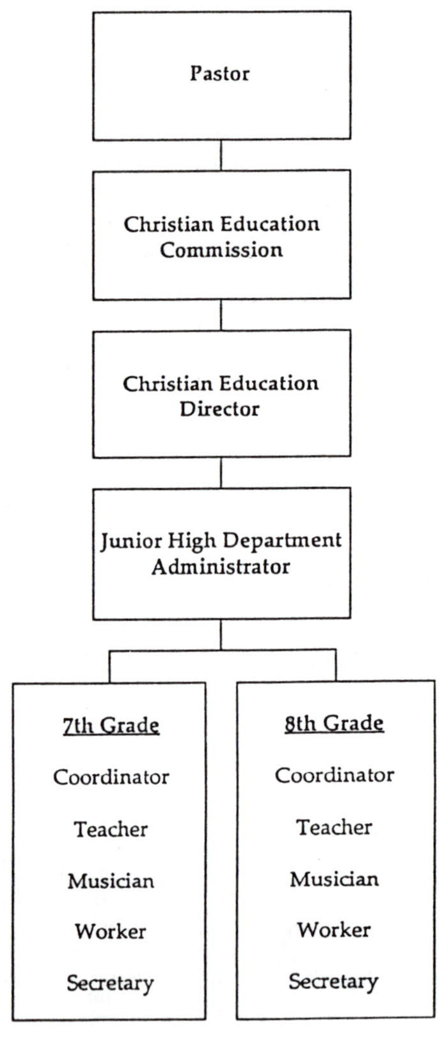

Pastor
Christian Education Commission
Christian Education Director
Junior High Department Administrator
7th Grade
Coordinator
Teacher
Musician
Worker
Secretary
8th Grade
Coordinator
Teacher
Musician
Worker
Secretary

Junior Department Flowchart

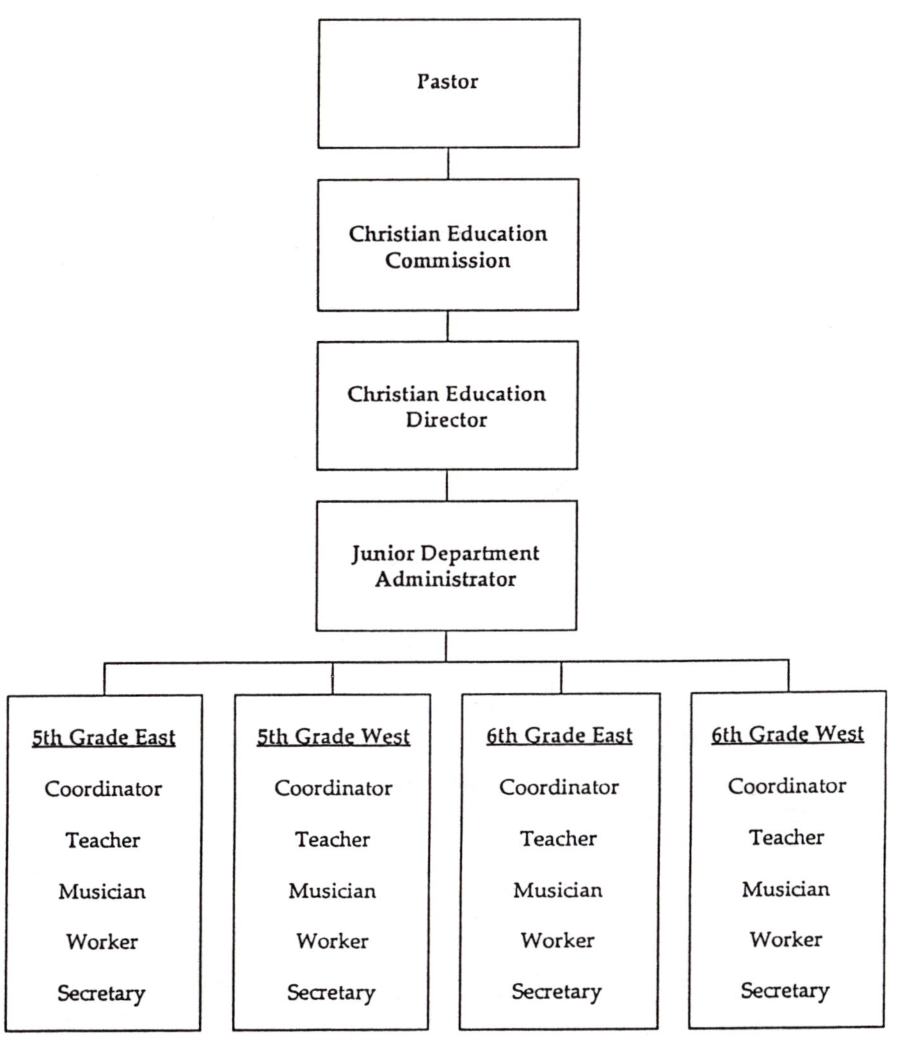

Middler Department Flowchart

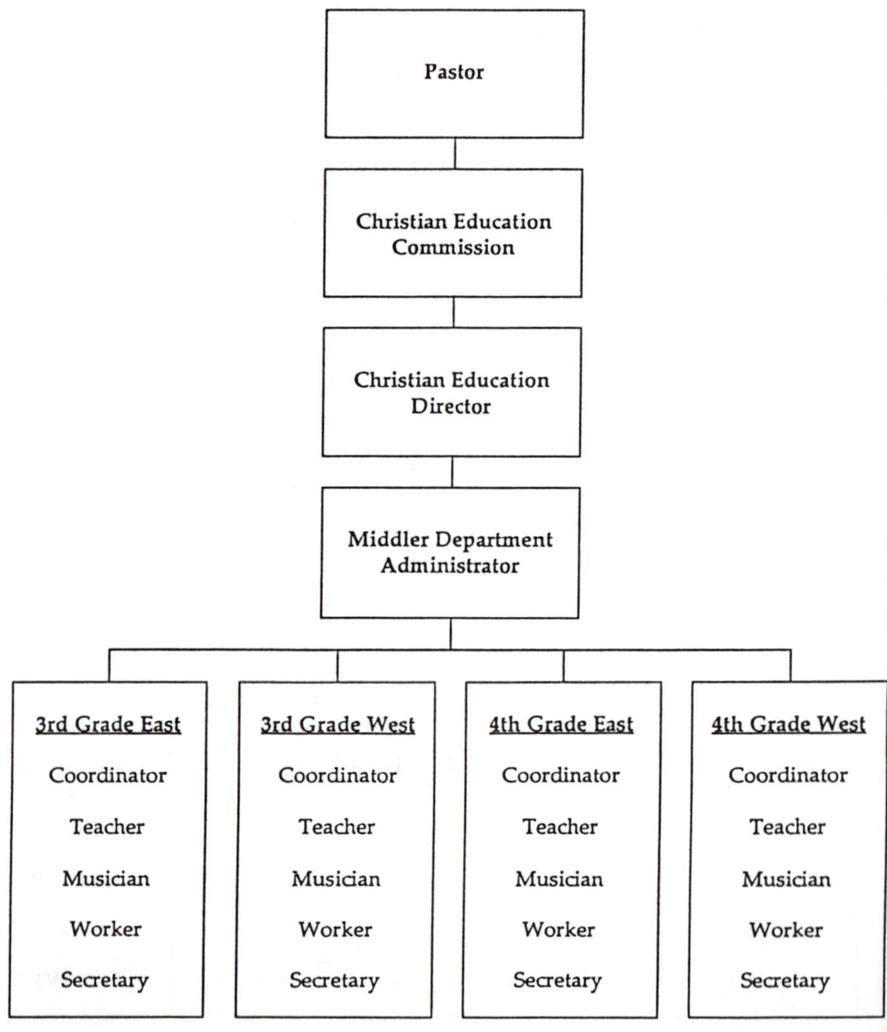

Primary Department Flowchart

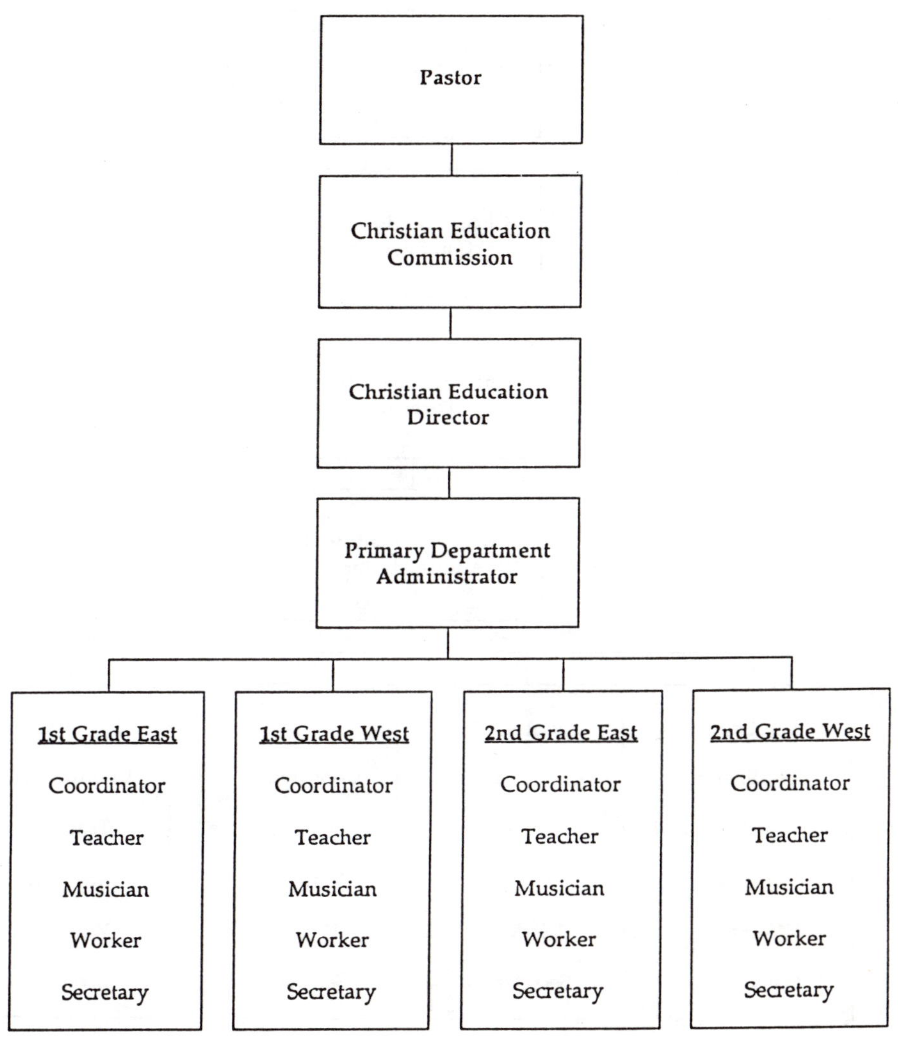

Preschool Department Flowchart

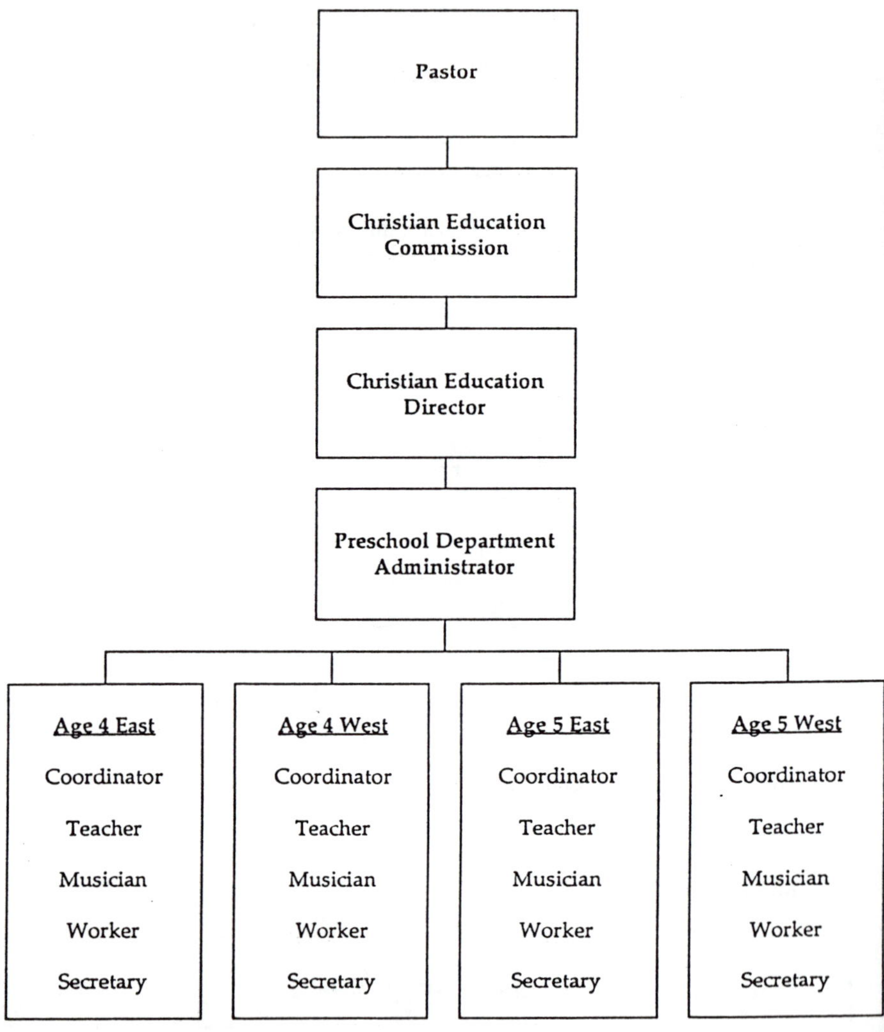

Nursery Flowchart

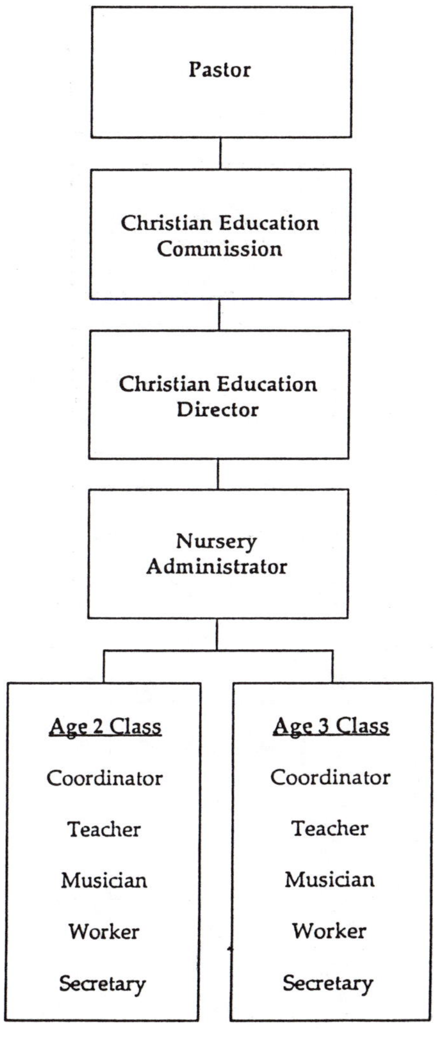

Toddler's Nursery Flowchart

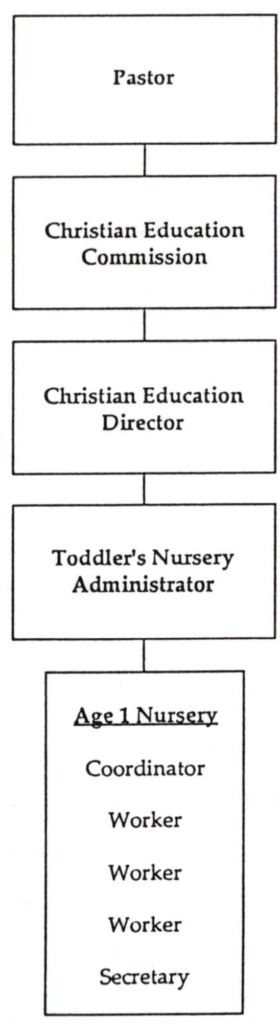

Infant Nursery Flowchart

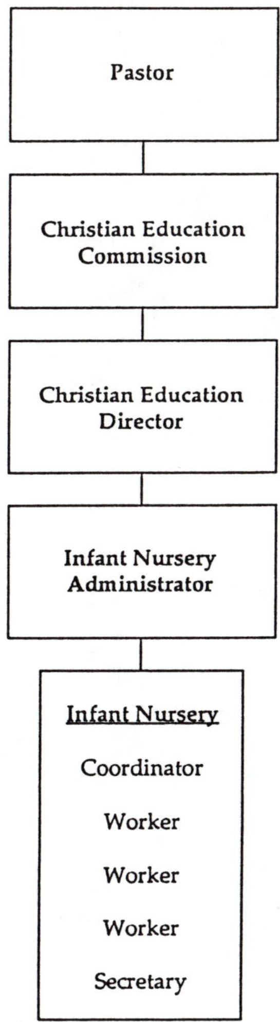

Job Descriptions

In this section of the book I will share job descriptions for various workers in the church school of the Bible.

Administrator

Job Description

The Administer is responsible for the overall function of a department of classes. He is to oversee and guide the Class Coordinators and Teachers toward an effective and fruitful team ministry, with a view to strengthen the families and the general ministry of the local church.

A. Supervision.

1. Oversee the Class Coordinators under your care.

2. Make certain every class has a leader present.

3. Encourage the workers to be punctual, neatly and appropriately dressed and friendly.

4. Be in the hall 30 minutes before the classes begin to greet the teachers and students as they arrive.

5. Check around to see if there are any physical problems with the building that need to be corrected before the class begins. (Roof leaks, electrical problems, etc.)

6. Be sensitive to encourage and pray for any of your teachers who are experiencing personal hardships.

7. Know each class team and be ready to step in and oversee a class if the Coordinator's post cannot be filled.

8. Make sure the records are being correctly handled, and that the offerings are getting to the Department Secretary with correct designations.

9. Take an active role in promotions to stimulate interest and growth in the classes.

B. Teacher Training.

1. Conduct regular training sessions for your teaching teams, either as a department, or in conjunction with other departments.

2. Make every member of the group aware of the specific teaching goals of the class, both long term and short term.

3. Share your ideas for improving the classes, and listen to others' ideas with respect and evident appreciation.

4. Encourage friendship and fellowship among the people in your department.

5. Discuss new materials and teaching aids available, and continually promote creativity, excitement, and the best audio-visual materials you can use.

6. Minister to the Class Coordinators under your supervision. Visit them as they visit those in their charge. Pray for and with them.

C. Discipline.

1. Be aware of any major discipline problems in the classes.

2. Be ready to handle any special discipline that the Coordinator cannot handle.

3. If a problem child is taken out of a class and given over to you for correction, be sure to make an effort to locate at least one of his parents before trying to make any corrections yourself.

4. NEVER spank or strike a child. Leave that up to the parents. Use physical restraint only if the child is a physical threat to someone.

If a child is a consistent source of disruption to his class, you may find it necessary to suspend him. But, realize that disruptive anti-social behavior is a sure indication of severe personal and spiritual problems. Make sure that child is visited several times at home by teachers or others who are competent to minister to families, unless the family declines the offer to help.

Class Coordinator
Job Description

The Coordinator is the leader of the teaching team in each classroom of the School of the Bible. He or she has the primary responsibility for the class and is directly responsible to the department Administrator.

A. Attend special leaders meetings.

1. Keep informed on current developments and programs that relate to your class.

2. Share ideas and information with other Coordinators.

3. Receive information, encouragement, and ideas from the Christian Education Director, Pastor, or Administrator.

4. Pray together.

5. Plan for the expansion and improvement of the School of the Bible ministry.

B. Supervise the training of the teaching team.

1. Class counsel meetings.

    a. Conduct a special meeting with all of your workers at least once each quarter.

    b. Discuss ideas for improvements in the class.

    c. Share information from the Coordinators' meetings that is relevant to your team.

    d. Discuss long term and short term goals for the class.

    e. Discuss and try to resolve any problems encountered in the class. Heal any interpersonal conflicts quickly.

    f. These meetings could be conducted in one of the homes, with fellowship or a shared meal.

2. Make assignments for responsibilities for each class session at least 10 days in advance.

a. Require each worker to report on the assignment plans and make sure their segment coordinates with the class theme.

b. Instruct them to obtain and prepare props and teaching aids ahead of time.

3. Lead the group in setting goals.

a. Attendance goals.
b. Offering goals.
c. Spiritual goals.
d. Visitation goals.

4. Lesson objectives.

a. Quarterly objectives: an outline of what you want to communicate for the quarter.
b. Unit objectives: usually a 4-week plan.
c. Weekly aim: the theme for this session.

5. Work with the team to plan special events, parties, field trips, service projects, etc.

a. Make specific assignments to share responsibilities.
b. Fill out and submit the activity form to the Christian Education Director.

6. Lead the team in prayer before the class begins each Sunday.

C. *The Coordinator is to help nurture the spiritual well-being of each member of the class.*

1. Know the students personally, and be sensitive to their emotional and spiritual needs.

2. Be prepared to counsel on a one-to-one basis, if needed.

3. Set a godly example in your personal lifestyle and disposition.

D. Supervise the care of the classroom.

1. Never use tape on the walls or windows. Never use nails or thumbtacks on walls. Use stick-tack, instead.

2. In rooms with drop ceilings, lightweight objects may be hung from the ceiling grids.

3. Remove outdated decorations.

4. Turn off the lights after class.

5. Make sure trash is picked up and put in the wastebasket.

6. Report maintenance problems to the office.

7. Clean the chalkboards. Never use water on a chalkboard.

8. Arrange the chairs neatly.

E. Storage Cabinet.

1. Clean out the closet frequently.

2. Do not store food in the room or cabinet. It will draw all sorts of insects.

3. Be conscious of the fire hazard of clutter.

F. Classroom discipline problems.

1. The Class Coordinator is responsible for handling any normal discipline problems in the class

with patience and consideration for the well-being of
the group.

     a. Never discipline a student with ridicule.

     b. Never strike a student.

     c. Convey love and acceptance while trying
to determine the reason for the uncooperative
or harmful behavior.

     d. If possible, take a disruptive student
aside and try to find out what his problem is,
being careful not to convey rejection, as "you're
a bad boy," or "I don't know what I'm going to
do with you."

     e. Never leave a student alone in the hall.

2. Severe discipline problems should be referred
to the child's father or mother if they are available.

     a. If a parent is not in the building, the
Administrator should handle to problem.

     b. The Administrator should call the par-
ents as quickly as possible.

     c. The Administrator should give the child
some personal attention and seek to discover
the real problem behind the behavior so he can
minister to the need.

***G. Coordinate and lead the visitation pro-
gram.***

1. Assign a few of the students to each worker on
the team.

2. Have each worker keep in touch with and continue to encourage all of the students to whom they
are assigned.

     a. Birthday cards.

b. Phone calls.

c. Visits in the home.

d. Regular prayer for each student.

3. Organize regular visitations to the students.

a. Select a specific day, and get brief, written reports.

b. Go with a new worker to show them how to make an effective home visit.

c. Make visitation an integral part of the Sunday School ministry program.

4. Be aware of absentees.

a. Make contact with missing students on a regular basis by writing, phone calls, and visitation.

b. If a student has been absent for more than 6 weeks, and every effort has been made to encourage them to return, then contact your Administrator for approval to remove their name.

c. No name should be removed without the Administrator's approval. It is the Coordinators' responsibility to keep track of extended absentees and not allow them to remain on the records if they have not indicated they will be returning soon.

d. Keep a record of the name, address, and phone number of each child whose name has been deleted and contact each one again at a later date, 3 months or sooner.

Teacher
Job Description

A. Communicate the Word of God to the hearts and spirits of your students. This involves:

1. Planning.

a. Think ahead.

b. What response do I want to stimulate in their hearts this week?

(1) What do I want them to know?

(2) What do I want them to feel?

(3) What do I want them to do?

c. Suggested goals:

(1) Cultivate gratefulness to God as Creator, Provider, and Protector.

(2) Lead students to repentance by awareness of sin, grace, faith.

(3) Combat the "me-centered" mentality of humanism and teach the joy of giving, serving, and preferring one another.

(4) War against a temporal values system, with an awareness of the second coming of Jesus, heaven, hell, eternity, and the judgment seat of Christ.

d. Biblical goals *(from II Peter 1:5-7)* in order:

(1) Faith.

(2) Virtue (character).

(3) Knowledge.

(4) Self-control.

(5) Godliness.

(6) Brotherly kindness.

e. What are the curriculum goals this year?

2. *Preparation:* This involves work through the week, preparing your heart as well as your mind.

a. Read the lesson materials you have and all the related Scriptures early in the week.

b. Incorporate Scriptures and materials from the lesson into your daily devotions through the week.

c. Create an introduction that will stimulate curiosity and interest.

d. Know the material thoroughly. Practice by discussing or even presenting the material to your family.

e. Look for, or make, props, pictures, or other visual aids which will captivate the student's interest and reinforce the message.

f. Have an introduction, main body, and a definite conclusion that will stimulate your students towards the lesson goal.

3. *Prayer.*

a. Prepare your spirit as a servant of God. Become sensitive to the will of God and be led by the Spirit.

b. Pray every day, on a regular basis, for each of your students by name, and for the needs you know about in their lives.

c. Learn from your students what their specific needs are, and let them know you are praying about those needs.

d. Keep notes about prayer needs.

e. In praying (privately and before the class):

(1) Always begin with thanksgiving (*"enter into His gates with thanksgiving, and into His courts with praise..." Psalm 100:4*).

(2) Pray to the Father in Jesus' name.

(3) Bless the Lord, and honor His name.

(4) Create a focus on His will, His kingdom, His purpose, and His pleasure.

(5) Make specific petitions for healing, provision, and spiritual growth based on His Word and purposes.

(6) Ask for His forgiveness for wrong attitudes and deeds and pray for overcoming grace as you come with a grateful and humble spirit. Do not recite prayers; talk to God. Pray in the Spirit; pray audibly whenever possible and have set times to pray.

Jesus gave His disciples a MODEL prayer, not one to recite, but one to emulate. Here is a similar model:

"Heavenly Father, thank You for loving us and for sending Your only Son, Jesus, to die on the cross for our sins. We love You, and appreciate all the wonderful things You have done in our lives. Thank You for bringing us together as a group to study Your Word and learn Your ways. Thank You for Jason, Sarah, Joey,...and for providing godly parents and a good church where we can worship You. Dear Lord, help us to understand more clearly what You are doing in our lives and what You want us to do with every precious day You give us to live.

Teach us to grow in Your love by loving and serving one another, and, today, let every one of us know without a doubt that we are born again, changed, and walking with the Lord Jesus Christ as our Savour and Lord. Help us to realize every day that Jesus is coming soon, and anoint us to worship You in everything we do, in Jesus' name, Amen."

(7) Start your day with the Bible reading and prayer.

(8) Include prayer at mealtimes and family devotions.

(9) Pray together and minister to one another as a teaching team before the class.

(10) Teach the children to pray for each other, or for a leader who has a serious need.

4. Personality.

a. Communicate the Word with joy, conviction, and confidence. NEVER read a book to your class, other than a Bible.

b. Look at the students and be sensitive to their response.

c. Call the students by name often and encourage them to ask questions. They are more important than your presentation.

5. Persuasiveness.

a. Know what this church believes.

b. Be able to overcome the mental roadblocks that have been established in the students' minds by the world.

6. Punctuality. Arrive 30 minutes early so you can quiet your heart and help greet the students.

B. Share the responsibility for instruction in at least one of these teaching segments:

1. Bible story.
2. Object lesson.
3. Life-related story.
4. Scripture memorization.

C. Learn to use a variety of teaching techniques and aids effectively.

1. Animate your lecture with body language, illustrations, props, and questions.
2. Flannel graph.
3. Overhead transparency projector.
4. Video Cassette player.
5. Puppets.
6. Skits with costumes and props.
7. Chalk drawings.
8. Songs that tell or punctuate the story.

D. Learn the material in advance.

1. NEVER read a story or carry a quarterly.
2. Do not try to show pictures from a book to a class. Books were made to be used by individuals, not groups.

E. Carry and read only a Bible.

    1. Make the Bible visible.

    2. Encourage the students to bring their Bibles with them and use them if they are able to read.

    3. Always teach a lesson or tell a story in your own words.

F. Pray daily for the students and for the Sunday class session.

G. Greet the students. Make them feel welcome and loved.

H. Be sensitive to special needs and problems.

I. Honor the Class Coordinator as the team leader by giving him or her your full support and cooperation.

J. Be ready to substitute for the Class Coordinator when called upon to do so.

K. Attend at least 48 Sunday School sessions each year.

L. Be a faithful tither to this local church.

M. Attend at least two other regular services at this church each week to strengthen your own spirit.

N. Participate in the visitation ministry program for your class. Realize that the students' parents are very important to the success of your ministry.

O. Attend Sunday School workers meetings and training sessions as provided to develop and enhance your skills and team spirit.

P. Be supportive of the overall vision and ministry of the church.

1. Always be aware that we need each other.

2. The goal of a true servant is to make others successful.

3. We are a team!

Q. Be an example of Christian purity and love.

1. Live the lifestyle you teach to your students.

2. Be quick to forgive and resolve offenses and misunderstandings, especially with brothers and sisters in the church.

R. Always contribute to the offering to set an example.

S. Teach the use of offering envelopes.

T. DO NOT USE SECULAR MATERIAL:

1. Secular music lyrics.

2. Secular films (even though they may seem so "nice.")

3. Secular books. Expose your class to Christian heroes and stories which put God in the perspective.

U. Be careful to put nothing on the walls except in designated areas.

V. Help keep the room and closets clean.

W. Turn out the lights when you leave the classroom.

Musician

Job Description

A. Strengthen the message and impact of the class session with good, appropriate music.

1. Planning.

a. Work with the Song Leader and Teacher in choosing songs prayerfully which will flow with and reinforce the objectives of the lessons.

b. Know the lesson plan and have the song list several days in advance of Sunday.

c. Keep looking for new songs which are biblical and fun to sing, particularly action songs.

d. Refer to the song list in the manual.

2. Preparation.

a. Make sure you know the correct keys and chord progressions for the songs. You may need to consult one of the senior musicians during the week.

b. Practice the songs; get some coaching, if necessary.

c. Practice the songs with the Song Leader.

3. Prayer.

a. Prepare your spirit as a servant of God.

b. Become sensitive to the will of God and be led by the Spirit.

4. Playing.

a. Adjust your instrumental volume to the size of the room and the size and age of the group.

b. For 10 to 12 first graders, you need to play softly.

c. Do not play with your back to the Song Leader or group, especially if you play the guitar.

d. Play with skill and anointing.

B. Support the teaching team with your presence and help during the entire class time.

1. Be ready to play at other times during the class as needed for an altar call, special song, etc.

2. Smile.

C. If you must be absent, contact a substitute during the week and notify the Class Coordinator.

1. Be sure the substitute is approved by the Administrator and Class Coordinator.

2. Make sure the Coordinator has the phone number of at least one substitute on hand in the event an unforeseen circumstance would keep you out of the class.

D. Honor the Class Coordinator as the team leader by giving him or her your full support and cooperation.

E. Attend at least 48 Sunday School sessions each year.

F. Be a faithful tither to this local church.

G. Attend at least two other regular services at this church each week to build up your own spirit.

H. Be supportive of the overall vision and ministry of the church.

1. Always be aware that we need each other.

2. The goal of a true servant is to make others successful.

3. We are a team!

I. Be an example of Christian purity and love.

1. Live the lifestyle you teach about.

2. Be quick to forgive and resolve offenses and misunderstandings, especially with brothers and sisters in the church.

Worker

Job Description

The general worker is the most flexible member of the teaching staff. He is an assistant to the Class Coordinator, the Secretary, and the Teacher. He may be in training for a teaching ministry, or may be one who has a vision for the program, but does not feel called to carry the full responsibility as the leader. He may be called to the ***"ministry of helps,"*** mentioned by Paul in I Corinthians 12. If so, he is likely to be greatly appreciated in a day when few people are really willing to be a true servant to others.

A. Assist the Secretary

1. Know the records procedures, and be able to handle the work, when needed.

2. Help with attendance, offering, etc.

3. Assist the Coordinator and Teachers. Be available and willing to teach and to assist with special promotions and events.

B. Help maintain discipline in the class with firm but loving sensitivity to any disruptions.

C. Participate in the visitation program.

D. Attend the scheduled training sessions and planning meetings scheduled.

E. Be active in praying for the class, the individual students, and for the ministry team.

F. Relate personally to the students whenever possible.

G. Come 30 minutes before the class begins and stay through to the dismissal time; participate in the singing, prayer, and activities; and support each of the team members.

H. If you must be absent, notify the Class Coordinator as soon as possible.

I. Honor the Class Coodinator as the team leader by giving him or her your full support and cooperation.

J. Attend at least 48 Sunday School sessions each year.

K. Be a faithful tither to this local church.

L. Attend at least two other regular services at this church each week to build up your own spirit.

M. Be supportive of the overall vision and ministry of the church.

1. Always be aware that we need each other.

2. The goal of a true servant is to make others successful.

3. We are a team!

N. Be an example of Christian purity and love.

1. Live the lifestyle you teach about.

2. Be quick to forgive and resolve offenses and misunderstandings, especially with brothers and sisters in the church.

Secretary

Job Description

A. Greet each student and help create an atmosphere of love and joy in the house of the Lord.

1. Learn each student's name as quickly as possible, and call them by name often.

2. Always recognize visitors and show a special interest in them.

3. Make name tags for the students.

4. Collect the tags at the end of the class and use them again every Sunday.

5. Introduce each new student to a worker.

6. Help make the students feel special about themselves.

7. Keep track of birthdays and, before the session, inform the Class Coordinator of current ones. Send cards to students with birthdays the following week.

8. Keep a list of absentees for visitation, cards, and calls.

B. Keep accurate records of each class session.

1. Attendance

    a. Use the computer attendance sheet; mark a <u>black</u> letter "P" for present and a <u>red</u> "A" for absent.

    b. For a new student who has just become a regular attender, fill out the **blue change sheet** with the class and department, the student's name, address, telephone number, birthday, parents' name and previous dates attended. A student is a "regular" when he or she has attended at least three times in a consistent manner, e.g., once a month for several months, every other Sunday, etc. Place a blue sheet inside the attendance sheet when finished.

    c. Fill out or update a **yellow visitor's form** with name, address, telephone number, birthday, parent's names, and date attending. Continue to record the dates attended on this sheet until the visitor becomes a regular. Keep the yellow form in the file box with the white permanent cards.

d. Total the number of class members and visitors and record it at the bottom of the computer attendance sheet.

e. Take the completed attendance folder and offering envelope to the Divisional Secretary's office and check it over with the secretary.

f. Be sure you have a permanent information card for each student on your attendance sheet.

2. Offering

a. The secretary is responsible for counting the School of the Bible offering and putting it in the envelope provided.

b. Record the total amount for the day on the envelope.

c. Record the total attendance on the envelope.

d. Keep any specially designated offerings separate and turn them into the Divisional Secretary with a note of explanation.

e. Take the completed attendance folder and offering envelope to the Divisional Secretary's office, check it over with the Secretary.

3. Maintenance record keeping

a. Always check the computer visitation sheet for correct information. There may be a change of address or telephone number.

b. If a student tells you of a change of address or telephone number, fill out the **blue change sheet,** put it inside your attendance sheet and turn them in to the Divisional Secretary.

    c. Keep the visitation sheet each week for reference.

    d. Keep the birthday sheet which you will receive monthly. Fill in any birthdays not listed and turn them in on a **blue change sheet.**

    e. Be sure to have a white permanent information card for each student on your computer attendance sheet and keep it in your file box. Do not forget to fill out a card for a visitor who becomes a regular attender. (Discard the yellow visitor's form.)

4. Other records

    a. During some promotions, records may be kept on separate forms relating to memory work, recruiting, or points for special efforts.

    b. Occasionally, you may need some assistance from another worker to keep these extra records straight.

    c. If an instruction sheet is delivered with additional paperwork, keep it in your attendance folder during the promotion and follow the instructions on the page.

C. *Follow-Up.*

1. Write out ***welcome cards*** for new students.

    a. Cards may be obtain from the Audio-Visual Room.

b. Include a little personal note. Be sure to sign your name and grade level. Do not just write "secretary."

c. Address the cards.

d. Take the cards to the Audio-Visual Room to be mailed.

2. Absentee follow-up.

a. One Sunday missed: send a "miss you" postcard.

b. Two Sundays missed: give the student's name and phone number to a Teacher or to the Class Coordinator so a phone call can be made that week.

c. Three Sundays missed: Make sure the student is visited by a Teacher or by the Coordinator.

3. Decision Cards.

a. These cards are available in the Audio-Visual Room.

b. Fill out one card for each student who responds to the salvation appeal in a class session and turn it in to the Administrator.

c. Put the date and the student's name on the "Spiritual Life" form.

4. The books should be turned into the Divisional Secretary no later than 30 minutes after the beginning of class.

THREE REQUIREMENTS FOR EVERY TEACHER

The Bible has a great deal to say about teachers. Teaching is one of the special types of ministries that Christ Himself has placed in the church as a **"gift."** Read carefully the following Scripture portion.

"And he gave some, apostles; and some, prophets; and some, evangelists, and some, pastors and teachers; for the perfecting of the saints, for the work of the ministry, for the edifying of the body of Christ: Till we all come in the unity of the faith, and of the knowledge of the Son of God, unto a perfect man, unto the measure of the stature of the fullness of Christ: That we henceforth be no more children, tossed to and fro, and carried about with every wind of doctrine, by the sleight of men, and cunning craftiness whereby they lie in wait to deceive; But speaking the truth in love, may grow up into him in all things, which is the head, even Christ: From whom the whole body fitly joined together and compacted by that which every joint supplieth, according to the effectual working in the measure of every part, maketh increase of the body unto the edifying of itself in love."

Ephesians 4:11-16

We discover from these beautiful verses that the Lord places teachers in the church for the following purposes:

A. To perfect the saints.

B. For the work of the ministry.

C. To build up the body of Christ.

D. To help the church come into a unity of faith.

E. To give knowledge about the Son of God.

F. To exemplify a godly lifestyle.

G. To establish us in doctrine.

H. To prove the love of God.

I. To help believers fit into the body of Christ.

The work of the teacher is important. God demands that every teacher have:

A CALL (I Corinthians 12:26-28)

God calls people to be teachers and workers. The gifts and callings of God are without repentance. Once we are called, we do not have an option. God requires a called teacher to teach.

COMPASSION (Matthew 9:36-38)

"But when he saw the multitudes, he was moved with compassion on them, because they fainted, and were scattered abroad, as sheep having no shepherd. Then saith he unto his disciples, 'The harvest truly is plenteous but the laborers are few; pray ye therefore the Lord of the har-

vest, that he will send forth laborers into his harvest.'"

The Master Teacher was moved with compassion. Jesus cared. Jesus wept. Jesus was concerned, because He loved His people. He had something to give that would meet their needs. Every teacher needs to have the motivation and conviction that what he has is greatly needed by the people.

When we genuinely give our heart to the Lord Jesus Christ, it naturally translates into a love for people. In loving Jesus, we please Him, we become like Him, and our motivations become more and more like His. Jesus was motivated by a supreme devotion to the Father, and by a selfless love for people. He was the consummate servant: He did nothing out of a motivation for self-gratification or self-glory.

COURAGE (Joshua 1:1-16)

God spoke words of encouragement to Joshua, who, in turn, encouraged the people to "be of good courage." The path to courage is to focus on God's Word and on what God has done, rather than focus on our abilities or accomplishments.

Compassion and courage go naturally together. The Apostle John said, *"there is no fear in love; but perfect love casteth out fear..." (I John 4:18).* Fear relates to the apprehension over potential loss. When we are a true servant and focus on the needs of others instead of ourselves, we are set free from fear and can boldly proclaim the Word of God. Daniel said, *"The people that do know their God shall be strong, and do exploits" (Daniel 11:32).* It takes courage to lead a class and bear the burden of ministering faithfully week after week.

Every teacher must know that he has a call from God and not just a desire to be in front of people. He must have a genuine compassion for people and a passion for souls, not just a desire to succeed in a ministry. Every teacher must also have the courage to do what needs to be done in the work, or he will give up when there are difficulties or conflicts.

Statement of Purpose

Youth Department High School Ministry

Evangelism

Youth Departments exist for the purpose of introducing teenagers to the gospel and receiving Jesus Christ as their Savior.

Establish

Youth Departments exist for the purpose of instructing teenagers in the teachings of the Lord so they may become mature disciples.

Equip

Youth Departments exist for the purpose of equipping teenagers for works of service in the ministry and in the community.

Youth Departments exist for the purpose of providing recreational activities for teenagers in a positive environment.

Youth Departments exist to evangelize, establish, and equip teenagers so they will become mature Christians and make an impact in their world for Jesus Christ--and enjoy themselves in the process.

Ministry Philosophy

A. High school ministry is an important mission for the church.

Research indicates that 80% of the people in America who become Christians do so before they graduate from high school. It is a goal of a Youth Department to communicate the gospel effectively at a time when the majority of people are still open to spiritual concerns.

The attitudes, habits, and decisions teenagers wrestle with in high school may affect their entire future. High school ministry must help teenagers learn to make wise choices so their future will be positive and exciting.

B. High school ministry must acknowledge and relate to the teen culture in order to effectively communicate the gospel.

The message of the gospel never changes, and its meaning must never be compromised. However, the methods of communicating the gospel may change with each new generation. It is imperative that the gospel be communicated with contemporary relevance to the teen culture. If the gospel is not presented in a way that relates to the world in which a teenager lives, tragically, the gospel may not be given another chance.

C. *High school ministry must strive for excellence.*

Teenagers often view church as archaic. Along with cultural relevance, a high school ministry must be committed to excellence in order to win the attention, interest, and respect of teenagers.

D. *High school ministry must be goal oriented.*

If a high school ministry is not moving in a specific direction, then it is difficult to evaluate its success and needs. It is important that realistic goals are planned in order to measure success and determine needs.

E. *There are various levels of spiritual interest and commitment among teenagers.*

Teenagers differ in their relationship with Jesus Christ. Some are eager to know Him, some are interested but not eager, others have only a passing interest, and a few have no interest. It is important the high school ministry meets teenagers where they are and gives them opportunities to grow in their relationship with Jesus Christ.

F. High school ministry must be built on a team principle and not on the gifts of one individual.

When a youth ministry grows, it is not possible for one leader to personally develop a relationship with each student. Other leaders must become involved in order for growth to continue and for discipleship to take place. If a ministry is built solely on the charisma of one leader--when the leader is gone--the ministry will dissolve.

G. High school ministry must continually evaluate its progress in order to determine effectiveness.

In order to maintain excellence, cultural relevance, and goal achievement, it is essential to have critical and continual evaluation of the ministry.

The job descriptions which follow detail the responsibilities of those involved in a Youth Department High School Ministry.

Youth Department Coordinator

The Coordinator is responsible for the overall management of the class and the spiritual well-being and discipleship of the students.

A. Develop a team of Youth workers who will help with all areas of the class ministry.

1. There is a general Youth Department job description for every Youth worker. However, it is the responsibility of each Coordinator to develop an indi-

vidual, tailor-made, job description for each Youth worker in the class.

2. See that the Youth workers perform their duties correctly and effectively.

3. Confer with the Administrator before adding new Youth workers to the class.

    a. Anyone interested in becoming a Youth worker must fill out a Youth Department Youth worker Information Sheet.

    b. The Administrator and Coordinator will meet with the person to discuss the Information Sheet and to communicate the kind of commitment that is needed for the job.

B. Follow the class curriculum plan.

1. If a change in curriculum is desired, a written proposal must be submitted to the Education Commission, expressing the need for the change.

2. Keep up to date on issues and events that are pertinent to teenagers.

C. See that the classroom is in good order before and after class.

D. Oversee the class follow-up program.

1. Implement the "Follow-Up Contest" for the class.

    a. The "Follow-Up Contest" is explained on the "Follow-Up Contest Sheet."

    b. Meet monthly with the Administrator to discuss the follow-up program.

2. See that the students receive at least one visit during the year.

3. See that the students are called on a regular basis.

E. Oversee class activities.

1. Provide at least two social activities for the class during the year.

2. Select two Activity Council members for the year.

        a. The Activity Council members are to help with class activities.

        b. The Activity Council members will represent the class for Youth Department activities.

3. A church insurance form must be filled out for each activity.

4. Make an effort to attend all Youth Department activities.

F. Attend the Coordinator's Meeting the first Sunday of each month.

1. Complete the "Class Monthly Update" evaluation form for the meeting.

2. The meeting is to evaluate class progress, problems, and goals.

G. Notify the Administrator as soon as possible if you are unable to attend class because of sickness, vacation, etc.

H. Attend the Youth worker prayer meeting every Sunday morning.

Youth Department Teacher

A. The Teacher is responsible for the class curriculum instruction.

1. Prepare and deliver the Bible lesson.

a. Become acquainted with a variety of teaching methods.

b. Continue to update and refine your teaching skills.

2. Use the class curriculum plan when preparing each lesson.

B. Fulfill the specific job responsibilities assigned by the Class Coordinator.

1. Help with activities, decorations, and class management.

2. You will know exactly what is expected.

C. Notice first-time visitors and greet them.

D. Help with follow-up. (Required.)

1. The specific follow-up requirements will be determined by the Coordinator.

2. The teacher must keep follow-up records which are to be given to the Coordinator each month.

E. Attend all class activities and make every effort to attend all Youth Department activities.

1. Notify the Coordinator when it is not possible for you to attend a class activity.

2. When possible, admission for a teacher at Youth Department activities is free.

F. Notify the Coordinator as soon as possible whenever you are unable to attend class because of sickness, vacation, etc.

G. Attend the Youth worker prayer meeting every Sunday morning.

Youth Department Worker

A. Assist the Coordinator in class each Sunday morning.

B. Fulfill specific job responsibilities assigned by the Coordinator.

1. These responsibilities may include helping with activities, decorations, class management, or secretarial work.

2. These responsibilities will allow the worker to know exactly what is expected.

C. Be capable of leading a small group.

D. Notice first-time visitors and greet them.

E. Help with follow-up programs.

1. The specific follow-up requirements will be determined by the Coordinator.

2. The worker must keep follow-up records which are to be given to the Coordinator each month.

F. Attend all class activities and make every effort to attend all Youth Department activities.

1. Notify the Coordinator as soon as possible whenever you are unable to attend a class activity.

2. When possible, admission for a worker at Youth Department activities is free.

G. Notify the Coordinator as soon as possible whenever you are unable to attend class because of sickness, vacation, etc.

H. Attend the Youth worker prayer meeting every Sunday morning.

Youth Department Secretary

A. Keep the class attendance, visitation, first-timer, and birthday records.

1. Each class has a secretarial folder which contains a computer attendance sheet, visitation sheet, birthday sheet, student update sheet, follow-up sheets, and first-timer cards.

2. This secretarial folder is kept in the Audio Visual Room and is to be returned there after each class.

B. Keep the attendance records for the class.

1. Each class has a computer attendance sheet which contains the names of all active, regular students.

a. Each Sunday, the Secretary will mark "P" for present or "A" for absent on the computer attendance sheet.

b. Until the Secretary becomes acquainted with the teenagers, it is best to have the students "sign-in" on an attendance paper passed around the class.

2. When the attendance is completely and carefully recorded (double-check it so no one is missed), take the secretarial folder to the Department Secretary.

3. At the beginning of class, take a "head count" of the total number of students, visitors and Youth workers in class.

a. Send this number to the Youth Department Secretary immediately.

b. The "head count" may be taken to the Department Secretary by a worker.

C. Keep the Coordinator informed of all student absenteeism.

1. Record on the "Telephone Follow-Up" sheet names of the students who were absent for the week.

2. Give the Coordinator the "Telephone Follow-Up" sheet each week.

3. Send a postcard to every student who is absent from class. How frequently a postcard is sent should be discussed with the Coordinator.

D. Keep all first-time visitor records.

1. When a first-timer visits, make sure the visitor fills out a Youth Department First-Time Information Card.

2. The first-timer's name and address should be recorded at the bottom of the computer attendance sheet.

3. All first-timer cards are to be given to the Youth Department Department Secretary.

4. If the first-timer visits three times within the next three months, inform the Coordinator.

    a. If the first-timer begins to attend regularly, place this student on the student attendance sheet.

    b. The student should be asked before being placed on the attendance sheet.

E. Keep the class attendance records up-to-date.

1. If a student does not attend class within a two-month period, this student should be taken off the attendance sheet.

2. The exceptions are those students who have to work or leave for summer vacation, etc.

3. No student may be removed from the attendance sheet unless the student has been contacted and the reason for being absent has been discovered and discussed.

F. Keep student addresses and phone numbers up-to-date.

1. Check and compare the visitation sheet with the attendance sheet periodically for address and phone number corrections.

2. Record changes in addresses or phone numbers on the student update sheet.

G. See that birthday cards are sent to each student on the attendance sheet.

1. A computer birthday sheet is provided for each class.

2. Have the Coordinator and Youth workers sign the birthday card before it is mailed.

3. Keep the Coordinator informed of upcoming birthdays.

H. Keep track of the number of postcards, birthday cards, and special letters which are sent out during the month.

1. There is no special sheet for this, so the secretary will have to keep track on a separate sheet.

2. These records are to be given to the Coordinator for the monthly "Follow-Up Contest."

I. Attend all class activities and make every effort to attend all Youth Department activities.

1. Notify the Coordinator as soon as possible whenever you are unable to attend a class activity.

2. When possible, admission for a secretary at Youth Department activities is free.

J. Notify the Coordinator as soon as possible whenever you are unable to attend class because of sickness, vacation, etc.

K. Attend the Youth worker prayer meeting every Sunday morning.

Youth Department Department Secretary

A. Record all the attendance records for the Youth Department classes.

1. Send a report of the total Youth Department attendance to the School of the Bible Secretary as soon as it has been calculated.

2. Receive the folders from all class Secretaries and give them to the school of the Bible Secretary.

3. Record on a department attendance sheet the attendance of all Youth workers, visitors and students. This sheet is located in the department secretarial folder.

B. Count and record the Sunday morning offering.

1. The offering is to be given to the School of the Bible Secretary.

2. Record the amount of the offering on the department offering sheet.

C. Notify the Administrator as soon as possible whenever you are unable to attend Sunday morning because of sickness, vacation, etc.

D. Attend the Youth worker prayer meeting every Sunday morning.

The High School Teacher

The most important asset in the Sunday School for high school students is the **Teacher.** This is foundational. Curriculum, schedule, follow-up, seating capacity, classroom decor, promotions and everything else is secondary and works to serve the central figure, the Teacher. Everything rests on the teacher's ability. No matter how excellent the administration, or how good the curriculum, or how conducive the room, if the teacher does not do the job, all is lost, or at least is rendered mediocre.

Many elements are needed for quality education; but, if an effective teacher is not at the helm, then the Sunday School will struggle to produce spiritual or numerical growth. Curriculum, classroom management, and such imperatives as follow-up are essential to an effective high school Sunday School. Yet, if a teenager does not enjoy the teacher, then it is unrealistic to expect regular attendance.

What are the qualities of a good teacher? There are hundreds of books and teaching manuals available to aid in effective teaching. The following two general principles are the most important.

First and foremost, **a teacher is a learner.** The best teacher is the best student. "I've taught this way for 25 years, and I'm not about to change now."

That person may have been a teacher, but no more. A teacher is a learner and is always looking for new or old methods to improve. Truth never changes, but methods of instruction and communication continue to evolve. What worked yesterday may not work today. Yet, it may work again tomorrow. Some may have the calling and talent, but if they fall to laziness or pride, they are a "castaway."

In Howard Hendricks exceptional book, ***Teaching to Change Lives,*** he notes the following:

"...experience does not necessarily make you better; in fact it tends to make you worse, unless it's evaluated experience.

The good teacher's greatest threat is satisfaction ---- failure to keep asking, 'How can I improve?' The greatest threat to your ministry is your ministry."

In John Milton Gregory's classic work, ***The Seven Laws of the Teacher,*** law number one is that the teacher must continually seek for growth. Any teacher, who is not willing to sharpen his skills will soon become a petrified pedagogue. A teacher must be a learner. A teacher must continually stretch for self-improvement.

In public education, a school teacher must procure a Master's Degree in Education. This is not optional. The degree is to be completed within five years of the date on which the person begins to teach. Then, every five years a teacher must complete at least two education courses to update his skills. In the Sunday School, too often, if a person can talk, they are allowed to teach. I realize some of the best teachers have no formal education. Yet, the Bible does say that the people of this world are often wiser in dealing with their own kind than are the people of the light. Could this be true in our educational process? Great teachers are great students. We must have great teachers.

Second, a Sunday School teacher must take an interest in the students' lives. This is critical. High school teenagers can see a million dollar light show at the concert on Saturday night. Why should they get excited about going to Sunday school? What does the church have to offer? Can we compete with the twinkle and glitter of the world? I do not think so. But we can care. God cares. We care. They will know we are Christians by our love. Teenagers will come to class when they know someone cares.

It would be unrealistic to expect a teacher to become intimately acquainted with every student. It is being interested and concerned that makes the difference. **A teacher must care.**

Caring can be measured in a very practical way: **follow-up.** A teacher who is unwilling to do follow-up does not care and is trying to feed an ego ---- or is lazy. Get out of teaching. There are seasons when ---- because of work, family or other pressures ---- follow-up is not achieved. This is the exception. **A called teacher will have a good follow-up program.**

Finally, if a person is willing to improve teaching skills and willing to care for students, this does not necessarily mean the person is called to teach.

Some people serve in the function of a teacher, but not in the calling. In other words, they are a faithful worker and are serving as a teacher, but they do not have the gift of making the Bible come alive. They serve in the function of a teacher, until a called teacher is able to take the class, or until they eventually get discouraged.

Someone may say, **"Well, God's Word never returns void."** This is correct. It can bore as well as bear fruit; it can harm as well as heal, if not used skillfully.

How does one know if a person is called to teach? Charles Spurgeon put it in very practical terms, **"If people are edified and encouraged, then pursue the calling. If people are wearied and bored, then pursue a calling elsewhere."** This is a good rule of thumb. I will add one more.

Perhaps, the easiest measurement to whether a person is called to teach can be answered by one very simple question. Can the person make a class grow? Or at least, can a person maintain class attendance? When a Sunday school teacher gets a new class, is the attendance level maintained over the course of the year? If the class drops in attendance, then something is awry. It may be that the teacher is not called to teach. Attendance may be the true test of a called Sunday school teacher. Can the person grow a class or at least maintain class attendance?

A Sunday school may have a prestigious heritage, but it is only as effective as its present teacher. We must have anointed teachers. We must find them or produce them at all cost. We must do everything we can to train, cultivate, and

133

establish those individuals who have the call to teach. The teacher is central to the education process. And, in my mind, there is no higher calling.

Ministry Training and Evaluation
Youth Department High School Ministry

A. Each Youth worker is given a job description outlining the specific responsibilities of the position.

B. Each Youth worker will be trained by the Administrator or the Coordinator.

C. Periodic training classes will be held for the Youth Department staff.

D. A Youth Department staff retreat is held annually. This retreat provides an opportunity for all the Youth workers to gather for a time of fellowship, information exchange, teaching, and ministry direction.

E. Each month, the Coordinators meet with the Administrator for the purpose of evaluating the ministry progress.

F. Semi-annual evaluations are given to the teenagers to receive their input into the ministry.

G. Semi-annual "Ministry Satisfaction" reviews are completed by all the Youth workers.

H. Impromptu feedback is welcomed by all in the course of interpersonal communication.

"Iron sharpeneth iron, so a man sharpeneth the countenance of his friend."
Proverbs 27:17

Mission Statement

Youth Department High School Ministry

A mission statement is to be filled out by every Youth worker in the Youth Department at the beginning of the year.

What are the objectives or long-term goals for your ministry during the year?

Examples:

Class Coordinator:

1. We will have an average attendance of 30 students by (date —————).

2. Every teenager in the class will be called each month.

Workers:

1. I will phone at least two students every week.

2. I will pray every day for the class.

3. I will start a small group this year.

My long term goals for this year are:

1. _______________________________________

____

____

2. _______________________________________

____

____

3. _______________________________________

____

____

4. _______________________________________

____

____

5. _______________________________________

____

____

6. _______________________________________

____

____

Follow-Up Contest

Youth Department High School Ministry

"Be thou diligent to know the state of thy flocks, and look well to thy herds."
Proverbs 27:23

The purpose of the follow-up contest is to have fun, to work diligently, to give congratulations, and to spark incentive into all of us to be better Youth workers.

A. Youth Department follow-up is implemented in eight areas which are as follows:

1. <u>Postcards:</u> Brief notes sent to teens to let them know we are thinking about them.

2. <u>Letter and Birthday Cards:</u> Individual letters sent to teenagers to encourage them.

3. <u>Mailers:</u> Form letters sent to the entire class.

4. <u>Phone calls:</u> Personal phone calls to check up on students and see how they are doing.

5. <u>Visitation:</u> Personal visits to teenagers to let them and their family know we are concerned about them. This also includes visits to extracurricular activities. It does not include seeing a student at a Youth Department activity or chance meetings at the grocery.

6. <u>Class activity:</u> An activity that is planned by the class.

7. <u>Class Youth worker meeting</u>: A planned meeting with the class Youth workers.

8. <u>Unplanned activity:</u> A spontaneous activity with three or more teenagers that took no planning.

B. Every time a Youth worker performs a follow-up responsibility, it is to be recorded. At the end of the month, the Coordinators record the total number of follow-up contacts on their <u>"Monthly update"</u> report. The class that did the most follow-

up will be declared the "Follow-up Winner of the Month." The recording procedure is as follows:

1. <u>Postcards and letters:</u> honor system.

2. <u>Mailers:</u> A copy of the letter must be handed in.

3. <u>Phone calls:</u> All Phone Call Follow-Up sheets must be handed in. No points, if no one was home!

4. <u>Visits:</u> All Visitation Follow-Up sheets must be handed in for points to be awarded.

5. <u>Activities:</u> A church insurance form is to be handed in.

6. <u>Youth worker meeting:</u> honor system.

7. <u>Unplanned activities:</u> honor system.

C. The points are calculated in the following manner:

1. Postcard = 1 point per card.

2. Letters/Cards = 3 point per card.

3. Mailer = 25 points per card.

4. Phone calls = 5 points per call.

5. Visit = 20 points per visit.

6. Class activity = 100 points per activity.

7. Youth worker meeting =50 points per meeting.

8. Unplanned activity = 50 points per activity.

SUGGESTED SCHEDULES FOR CLASSES

The following section will be suggested schedules for classes starting with the First Grade through the Sixth Grade.

FIRST GRADE CLASS SCHEDULE

8:35   Team prayer, greet students, student craft

9:05   Singing

9:13   Offering, announcements, birthdays, promos, etc.

9:21   Bible Lesson

9:29   Life-related story

9:37   Memory Verse

9:44   Catechism in Doctrine
(Systematic teaching with questions and answers)

9:52   Closing (altar call, song, prayer, pick up chairs)

10:00   Dismiss to parents

SECOND GRADE CLASS SCHEDULE

Super Sunday School Session

8:35	Team Prayer, Greet Students, Craft
9:05	Singing, Worship
9:12	Announcements, Offering, Birthdays, etc.
9:20	Bible Lesson
9:28	Object Lesson, or Project, etc.
9:36	Catechism Lesson
9:42	Scripture Memorization
9:50	Song
9:55	Prayer, Closing
10:00	Dismiss to General Service

THIRD GRADE CLASS SCHEDULE

Super Sunday School

8:35	Team Prayer, Greet Students, Craft
9:05	Singing, Worship
9:12	Announcements, Offering, Birthdays, etc.
9:20	Bible Lesson
9:28	Object Lesson, or Life-Related Story
9:36	Catechism
9:42	Scripture Memorization
9:50	Song
9:55	Prayer, Closing
10:00	Dismiss to General Service

FOURTH GRADE CLASS SCHEDULE

Sunday Morning Bible Class

8:35   Team Prayer, Greet Students, Craft

9:05   Singing, Worship

9:16   Announcements, Offering, Birthdays, etc.

9:22   Catechism

9:32   Object Lesson, or Project, etc.

9:42   Bible Lesson

9:55   Prayer, Closing

10:00   Dismiss to General Service

FIFTH GRADE CLASS SCHEDULE

8:35   Team Prayer, Greet Students, Fellowship

9:05   Singing, Worship

9:16   Announcements, Offering, Birthdays, etc.

9:22   Catechism

9:32   Object Lesson, or Project, etc.

9:42   Bible Lesson

9:55   Prayer, Closing

10:00   Dismiss to General Service

SIXTH GRADE CLASS SCHEDULE

Super Sunday School Session

8:35	Team Prayer, Fellowship, Greetings
9:05	Singing, Worship
9:16	Announcements, Offering, Birthdays
9:22	Catechism
9:32	Object Lesson, or Project, etc.
9:42	Bible Lesson
9:55	Prayer, Closing
10:00	Dismiss

The churches that are not growing will stagnate because sufficient time has not been given for laying a good foundation. Church growth cannot be sustained without careful and detailed planning. The structure of a church is the track upon which the church can run to success. Without a structural foundation, the church will not grow.

This is the MISSING ELEMENT in many churches across America.

When there is sincere preaching, earnest praying, dedicated workers, and detailed planning for building a strong foundation, the church of Jesus Christ will grow.

CHAPTER SEVEN

Understanding Your Students

In order to minister effectively to any group, it is imperative that you have a working knowledge of the people you teach. Their individual circumstance and personality will affect their response to you and your ministry. Please read this material carefully as you prepare your heart to minister in any capacity to some of the most important people in the world: **our children.**

We are concerned that you have a working knowledge of your students in a number of ways. Young people are complex. There are some principles that apply to children at specific age levels, and some that we can all relate to no matter what our age. There are also many variables that distinguish each one as unique, with special potentials, needs, and distinct problems. We are created body, soul, and spirit. Each part of our being is affected by our heritage, environment, and a vast array of cultural and social factors which affect our responses and reactions.

The profiles which follow describe a child's development at different ages. The more you understand about each child, the more effectively you will be able to handle his fears, misconceptions, and behavioral problems. These profiles will give you some general insights. You will also need to become familiar with such factors as family background, birth order, school influences, television habits, and family and personal devotional life. In doing so, you will have important resources available to minister to your students.

A Profile of First Grade Students

Physical Development

1. First grade students are growing unevenly and may be awkward. Be patient and quick to encourage them.

2. Their fine muscles are still being developed. It is best to avoid detailed craft work and activities that require fine motor skills.

3. They tend to be restless, with short attention spans. In addition, first graders usually have a large sugar intake, may have a lack of firm discipline, and probably have a high-impact, fast-paced television diet. To keep their attention, you must keep things moving. Limit class segments to eight minutes or less.

4. They are easily fatigued. Their bodies are still growing, their diet usually contains large amounts of sugar and fat, and they may not be getting enough exercise. As much as possible, alternate active and relaxed times in the class schedule.

5. First graders are losing their baby teeth. Show an interest in this important change.

6. They are susceptible to communicable diseases. Be alert to the general health of your students and instruct parents to keep sick children at home, until they are well.

Intellectual Development

1. First grade students are just learning to read. Do not require then read in class. Talk, sing, or learn scripture verses by rote.

2. They are in the process of developing their vocabularies. Be sure to explain words carefully and use words and phrases that are easily understood.

3. They are not able to think in analogies or abstract concepts. Focus on the basics and keep your explanations simple and straightforward.

4. First graders have keen senses and love to handle things. Use sight, touch and even taste, when possible.

5. They are very curious. Encourage questions and deal with them patiently.

6. They have good memories. Challenge the students to memorize larger portions of scripture.

7. They have good imaginations. Stimulate their imaginations. Let them act things out and talk. Teach students the difference between fantasy and vision.

Vision relates to hope and faith. Without a (spiritual) vision, people perish (become wild and undisciplined). Children need to be stimulated in a healthy imagination. To "pretend" and play is a major part of their development. They are able to begin to understand that there is a supernatural realm in God's creation, and that angels and demons are real.

Fantasy is a satanic counterfeit to vision. Fantasy focuses on inaccessible and impossible dreams that exalt the dreamer and feed off the selfish ego tendencies of the sin nature. There is much emphasis on "power" and self-glory. Today there is an avalanche of fantasy material ready to pour into the minds of children through television, humanistic books, and movies. The characters seem "good" and "so cute," but the message is demonic. Fantasy opens the mind to the occult and often leads to confusion, rebellion, depression, and suicide.

Social Development

1. First grade students have a great need for security. Teach them to trust in God, their parents, and the church.

2. They love appreciation and affection. Praise them, and give them hugs.

3. They are living in a peer-oriented culture. Teach them to relate to adults and to children of different age levels with respect and kindness.

4. They should enjoy talking. Encourage talking in turn. Draw out the reclusive students and listen attentively to what the students have to say.

5. First graders tend to be selfish. Teach them to share with others, to develop servant's hearts, and to be excited about blessing others.

6. They like to play with other children. Teach them the joy of sharing and caring.

7. They still respect authority, although, at this point, the respect may be eroding. Encourage and teach about respectful attitudes. Live worthy of respect yourself by showing respect for others.

Spiritual Development

1. First graders know right from wrong. Stimulate and encourage a healthy conscience.

2. They can know God and relate to spiritual things. Teach them to pray and to worship God.

3. They are curious about death. Help them understand about heaven, hell and eternity.

4. They can understand sin, faith, and repentance. Lead your students to genuine salvation.

NOTE: It is important to understand the difference between genuine salvation and religious conversion.

Religious conversion is an act of the mind and/or the emotions. A child raised in a Christian culture, which also teaches Santa Claus and other "cute" myths, tends to mix the images and messages in his mind and to think of God as a Santa. When he hears about God's love and desire to give to him, and about heaven, he will tend to think, "Sure. Why not?" He may learn the language, the motions and "accept" Jesus as part of his cultural background and weekly obligations without genuine repentance from sin and without making a covenant with God. He may notice in his teen years there is not much difference between him and the spirit he observes in the world, and decide that Christianity is "kid's stuff," like the Easter bunny and Santa's elves.

Genuine salvation is a work of the Spirit. It involves both faith and repentance. The Holy Spirit moves on the person's spirit (which includes the conscience) and "convinces of sin" while stirring in the heart the revelation of God's love and His holiness. We respond to the completed work of Christ on the cross with gratefulness and humility, recognizing our desperate need for forgiveness and healing. We respond to the covenant initiated by the shedding of His blood for us by giving our lives to Him, receiving Him both as Savior and Lord.

A Profile of Second Grade Students

Physical Development

1. Second grade students are growing unevenly and may be awkward. Be patient and quick to encourage them.

2. Their fine muscles are still being developed. It is best to avoid detailed craft work and activities that require fine motor skills.

3. They tend to be restless, with short attention spans. In addition, second graders usually have a large sugar intake, may have a lack of firm discipline, and probably have a high-impact, fast-paced television diet. To keep their attention, you must keep things moving. Limit class segments to eight minutes or less.

4. They are easily fatigued. Their bodies are still growing, their diet usually contains large amounts of sugar and fat, and they may not be getting enough

exercise. As much as possible, alternate active and relaxed times in the class schedule.

5. Second graders like to be doers. It is hard for them to sit and just listen for very long. Give them active things to do during the class time.

6. They should be somewhat talkative. Give the students opportunities to respond and encourage them to share their thoughts.

Intellectual Development

1. Second grade students are still learning to read. Be sensitive to each student's reading level. Have them read simple things as a group. Do not have students read solo, unless they volunteer.

2. They are in the process of developing their vocabularies. Be sure to explain words carefully and use words and phrases that are easily understood.

3. They are not able to think in analogies or abstract concepts. Focus on the basics and keep your explanations simple and straightforward.

4. Second graders have keen senses and love to handle things. Use sight, touch, and even taste, when possible.

5. They are very curious. Encourage questions and deal with them patiently.

6. They have good memories. Challenge the students to memorize larger portions of scripture.

7. They have good imaginations. Stimulate their imaginations. Let them act things out and talk. Teach students the difference between fantasy and vision.

Vision relates to hope and faith. Without a (spiritual) vision, people perish (become wild and undisciplined). Children need to be stimulated in a healthy imagination. To "pretend" and play is a major part of their development. They are able to begin to understand that there is a supernatural realm in God's creation, and that angels and demons are real.

Fantasy is a satanic counterfeit to vision. Fantasy focuses on inaccessible and impossible dreams that exalt the dreamer and feed off the selfish ego tendencies of the sin nature. There is much emphasis on "power" and self-glory. Today there is an avalanche of fantasy material ready to pour into the minds of children through television, humanistic books, and movies. The characters seem "good" and "so cute," but the message is demonic. Fantasy opens the mind to the occult and often leads to confusion, rebellion, depression, and suicide.

Social Development

1. Second grade students have a great need for security. Teach them to trust in God, their parents, and the church.

2. They love appreciation and affection. Praise them, and give them hugs.

3. They are living in a peer-oriented culture. Teach them to relate to adults and to children of different age levels with respect and kindness.

4. They should enjoy talking. Encourage talking in turn. Draw out the quiet students and listen attentively to what the students have to say.

5. Second graders tend to be selfish. Teach them to share with others, to develop servant's hearts, and to be excited about blessing others.

6. They are very concerned about fairness and it can be hard for them to take turns. Teach the students it is more important to give and prefer others to self. The focus on **"rights"** has come from the world, not from the Lord.

7. They still respect authority, although, at this point, the respect may be eroding. Encourage and teach about respectful attitudes. Live worthy of respect yourself by showing respect for others.

8. They prefer their own pals and tend to reject negatively to members of the opposite sex. Teach the students to relate to the opposite sex with respect and kindness, as friends.

9. They are concerned with being a winner, and being at the top. Teach them the Christian ethic of being servants. Contrast the beatitudes with the world's concept of who is **"blessed."**

Spiritual Development

1. Second graders know right from wrong. Stimulate and encourage a healthy conscience.

2. They can know God and relate to spiritual things. Teach them to pray and worship God. Also teach them about the gifts of the Spirit and other important doctrines.

3. They are curious about death. Help them understand about heaven, hell and eternity.

4. They can understand sin, faith, and repentance. Lead your students to genuine salvation.

NOTE: It is important to understand the difference between genuine salvation and religious conversion.

Religious conversion is an act of the mind and/or the emotions. A child raised in a Christian culture, which also teaches Santa Clause and other "cute" myths, tends to mix the images and messages in his mind and to think of God as a Santa. When he hears about God's love and desire to give to him, and about heaven, he will tend to think, "Sure. Why not?" He may learn the language, the motions and "accept" Jesus as part of his cultural background and weekly obligations without genuine repentance from sin and without making a covenant with God. He may notice in his teen years there is not much difference between him and the spirit he observes in the world, and decide that Christianity is "kid's stuff," like the Easter bunny and Santa's elves.

Genuine salvation is a work of the Spirit. It involves both faith and repentance. The Holy Spirit moves on the person's spirit (which includes the conscience) and "convinces of sin" while stirring in the heart the revelation of God's love and His holiness. We respond to the completed work of Christ on the cross with gratefulness and humility, recognizing our desperate need for forgiveness and healing. We respond to the covenant initiated by the shedding of His blood for us by giving our lives to Him, receiving Him both as Savior and Lord.

A Profile of Third Grade Students

Physical Development

1. Third graders are still growing, but are not as awkward as they were last year.

2. Their fine muscles are more developed and they have more coordination, now. Challenge the students to draw and work with crafts and music.

3. They still tend to be restless. Their muscles are still developing, many will have a large sugar intake, some may have a lack of firm discipline and many have a high-impact, fast-paced television diet. Keep things moving in the classroom. Limit segments to nine minutes or less.

4. Third graders can work, but often become impatient with their progress. Give clear directions and keep the students active. Praise them for their accomplishments.

5. They like to be doers. It is hard for them to sit and just listen for very long. Be sure to have active things for them to do.

6. They should be somewhat talkative. Give the students opportunities to respond and encourage them to share their thoughts.

7. The girls are maturing faster than the boys. Be careful not to emphasize size or physical maturity. Instead, place an emphasis on character.

Intellectual Development

1. Third grade students are probably acceptable readers. Be sensitive to each student's reading level. Have them read passages as a group.

2. They are in the process of developing their vocabularies. Be sure to explain words carefully and use words and phrases that are easily understood.

3. They are not able to think in analogies or abstract concepts. Focus on the basics and keep your explanations simple and straightforward.

4. Third graders have keen senses and love to handle things. Use sight, touch and even taste, when possible.

5. They are very curious. Encourage questions and deal with them patiently.

6. They have good memories. Challenge the students to memorize larger portions of scripture.

7. They have good imaginations. Stimulate their imaginations. Let them act things out and talk.

8. They are able to understand more abstract concepts and discover truth by reading. Encourage the students to read the Bible daily for themselves, and to use a simple, but honest translation.

9. They are beginning to think more in terms of a corporate view of life rather than seeing only themselves. Encourage a Christ-centered world view, rather than a self-centered world view.

10. They are beginning to see that there are many opinions on every subject. Teach them that, while everyone has their own ideas, the truth is in Jesus and the Bible, not in popular consensus.

Social Development

1. Third grade students are more secure in themselves, especially if they are in a strong and loving family. Teach students to gain their security and peace from God.

2. They love appreciation and affection. Praise them, and give them hugs.

3. They are living in a peer-oriented culture. Teach them to relate to adults and to children of different age levels with respect and kindness.

4. They may be caught up in teasing, jesting and name-calling. Teach them the importance of kindness and the power of the tongue to heal or hurt.

5. Third graders tend to be selfish. Teach them to share with others, to develop servant's hearts, and to be excited about blessing others.

6. They are very concerned about fairness and it can be hard for them to take turns. Teach the students it is more important to give and prefer others to self. The focus on "rights" has come from the world, not from the Lord.

7. They still respect authority, although, at this point, the respect may be eroding. Encourage and teach about respectful attitudes. Live worthy of respect yourself by showing respect for others.

8. They prefer their own pals and tend to reject or react negatively to members of the opposite sex. Teach the students to relate to the opposite sex with respect and kindness as friends.

9. They are concerned with being a winner, and being at the top. Teach them the Christian ethic of

being servants. Contrast the beatitudes with the world's concept of who is **"blessed."**

Spiritual Development

1. Third graders know right from wrong. Stimulate and encourage a healthy conscience.

2. They can know God and relate to spiritual things. Teach them to pray and to worship God. Also teach them about the gifts of the Spirit and other important doctrines in the Bible.

3. They are curious about death. Help them understand about heaven, hell and eternity.

4. They can understand sin, faith, and repentance. Lead your students to genuine salvation.

NOTE: It is important to understand the difference between genuine salvation and religious conversion.

Religious conversion is an act of the mind and/or the emotions. A child raised in a Christian culture, which also teaches Santa Claus and other "cute" myths, tends to mix the images and messages in his mind and to think of God as a Santa. When he hears about God's love and desire to give to him, and about heaven, he will tend to think, "Sure. Why not?" He may learn the language, the motions and "accept" Jesus as part of his cultural background and weekly obligations without genuine repentance from sin and without making a covenant with God. He may notice in his teen years there is not much difference between him and the spirit he observes in the world, and decide that Christianity is "kid's stuff," like the Easter bunny and Santa's elves.

Genuine salvation is a work of the Spirit. It involves both faith and repentance. The Holy Spirit moves on the person's spirit (which includes the conscience) and "convinces of sin" while stirring in the heart the revelation of God's love and His holiness. We respond to the completed work of Christ on the cross with gratefulness and humility, recognizing our desperate need for forgiveness and healing. We respond to the covenant initiated by the shedding of His blood for us by giving our lives to Him, receiving Him both as Savior and Lord.

A Profile of Fourth Grade Students

Physical Development

1. In terms of physical health, fourth graders are probably at their peak in life. This should be a happy age, with little responsibility, but with growing awareness of life and ability to participate in it.

2. Their motor skills are developing, and they are at the prime age to begin music lessons or learn skills in art or sports.

3. They need hard physical activity, although the only practical way for a Sunday School teacher to contribute here is either to encourage him to be active or to have an occasional activity outside of the class time.

4. Fourth graders are usually outgoing and sometimes loud. They need to be involved in discussions, as well as activities. It is difficult for them to sit quietly and listen to you talk for any length of time. Class segments should be limited to 9 or 10 minutes,

with a definite change of pace, leader, and/or direction each time.

5. The girls are ahead of the boys in physical maturity, but they can be fairly even with most kinds of competition. Unless the ratio is unusually lopsided, it is usually safe to group the "girls against the boys" for some light competition, as long as we make sure to maintain respect and kindness for everyone.

6. In America, many of our children are television addicts, sitting for hours a day. This not only steals much of their valuable learning time, but also damages them physically with a lack of exercise and the promotion of junk foods. Try to stimulate them toward more productive activities, such as music, sports, reading, and family devotions.

Intellectual Development

1. Fourth graders are probably acceptable readers by now. However, you still need to be careful about some who are slower than the others and who would be embarrassed to be called on to read individually.

2. Their vocabularies are growing. Know what words they understand, and try to teach them the meaning of at least one or two new words each week. Make sure you know the meaning of the words yourself. If you use a King James Bible, you need to realize that many words have changed in their meaning in the past 400 years or so. So, be careful. Words like "conversation," "quick," and "minister" have changed in the way they were used during that time. Words are extremely important. The way you define a word,

like "grace," or "remission," can dramatically affect the way you respond to life and to God.

3. Encourage them to ask questions. In fact, a good teacher will direct the class session to stimulate the student's thinking to the point where they will ask questions, and then they will be their most attentive. Also, ask questions, and avoid asking for "anyone" to answer. Usually, the same few will give answers, and some will never volunteer a response. Be careful when students give wrong answers to your questions. It is very important to correct errors without making a student look or feel foolish or embarrassed.

4. They are probably being exposed to many humanistic ideas, such as the doctrine of evolution and situational ethics. Teach them that the fear of the Lord is the beginning of knowledge, and that truth comes from God, and not from man's intellect.

5. They may be starting to feel the Bible is simple, and "kid's stuff," because the have heard the same stories in other classes. Do not be afraid to challenge their minds with deeper truths or less familiar Bible illustrations. It is healthy for children to see that there is more to learn and understand about the Bible, and to have a sense of wonder and awe about God.

Social Development

1. Fourth grade students are more confident, assertive, and outgoing than younger children, although some of them probably have some difficult circumstances. Those who are extremely unresponsive or overly obnoxious usually come from homes with spiritual problems. A good leader will be sensi-

tive to special needs or problems and seek to help, rather than react to the child as a "troublemaker."

2. They prefer the members of their own sex. Some boys may even be into "girl-hater" clubs. While we know that this usually changes in a few years, we need to address the issue of love and kindness and lead them into a healthier response to one another.

3. Their world is expanding, but they still tend to be selfish. This translates into an undue emphasis on "fairness." Teach them the principles of giving and sharing, and of sowing and reaping. Let them know that life is not fair, and that as Christians, our goal is to bless others, not to "get our fair share."

4. Children in the fourth grade are learning to tease and treat each other unkindly, and they may take advantage of smaller children. Teach them the power of the tongue to heal or to hurt, and the basic Christian ethics that relate to the hurting or the helpless. The church has been too tolerant of the "practical" joker, who derives pleasure from the hurt or embarrassment of someone else.

5. They need to be taught by precept and by example to respect authority, and to be encouraged to relate to and rely on their parents more. This is especially true in a time when parents are seriously ridiculed by a very powerful entertainment, which basically opposes Christian values and morality.

6. Lead your students away from the peer-oriented focus in our society and toward a more family-centered lifestyle. Seek to influence their parents to spend more quality time with them.

Spiritual Development

1. If a fourth grader has been in Sunday School for several years, he has heard many lessons and many appeals for salvation. It is important for the teacher to be aware of the spiritual condition of the students and of their Christian background, or lack of it. If there are some unsaved young people in the group, there will be times which are conducive for an **"altar call,"** or at least a question about their spiritual condition to be followed up later. If only one or two children have not made a confession of faith, rather than single them out and focus the entire group on their need, why not meet with them or their family later, and lead them to the Lord? It would probably be much more meaningful to them, and would prevent a few possible problems.

If we have an altar call every week for **"churched"** children.

a. They will tend to develop the idea that the salvation experience is all there is to Sunday School, and not keep a learner's heart later on. They may be more likely to drop out, with the idea that "I already got saved; several times, in fact. I don't need to go back."

b. There will be an embarrassing focus on one or two who are known to be new or unsaved.

c. We will miss opportunities to lead them to other experiences or character development. This is a good age for them to receive the baptism in the Holy Spirit, or to learn serving and giving.

d. It will get to be a ritual (rut), and lose its effectiveness.

Listen to the Holy Spirit to know when to make a spiritual appeal for salvation.

2, The spirit of a fourth grader is able to respond to spiritual truths, but perhaps his mind cannot fully grasp them yet. Use analogies and keep teaching and praying. The Holy Spirit is able to make truth come alive in his spirit and his understanding.

3. They should understand the significance of water baptism, and should be encouraged to be buried in the waters of Christian baptism.

4. They need to be led to respond in the Spirit, and not just focus on the social and intellectual aspects of life and religion. They should be able to hear from God and respond to Him.

NOTE: It is important to understand the difference between genuine salvation and religious conversion.

Religious conversion is an act of the mind and/or the emotions. A child raised in a Christian culture, which also teach Santa Claus and other "cute" myths, tends to mixthe images and messages in his mind and to think of God as Santa. When he hears about God's love and desire to give to him, and about heaven, he will tend to think, "Sure. Why not?" He may learn the language, the motions and "accept" Jesus as part of his cultural background and weekly obligations without genuine repentance from sin and without making a covenant with God. He may notice in his teen years there is not much difference between him and the spirit he observes in the world, and decide that Christianity is "kid's stuff," like the Easter bunny and Santa's elves.

Genuine salvation is a work of the Spirit. It involves both faith and repentance. The Holy Spirit moves on the person's spirit (which includes the conscience) and "convinces of sin" while stirring in the heart the revelation of God's love and His holiness. We respond to the completed work of Christ on the cross with gratefulness and humility, recognizing our desperate need for forgiveness and healing. We respond to the covenant initiated by the shedding of His blood for us by giving our lives to Him, receiving Him both as Savior and Lord.

A Profile of Fifth Grade Students

Physical Development

1. Fifth graders are usually strong and healthy, and love physical activity. If possible, give them, opportunities for recreation and exercise. Try to play extra outdoor activities.

2. They are developing motor skills rapidly, and should be increasingly skilled in crafts and music. They should be encouraged to develop skills in music or art, as well as sports.

3. They are usually not too tidy, and many need to be reminded occasionally to be neater in their appearance and in the care of the room.

4. Some of the girls are already maturing physically, and are taller than the boys. This is an awkward time for both sexes. We need to be careful not to draw attention to it, unless we gently mention in a general sense, that this is only temporary. Large girls and small boys are especially sensitive. Be careful.

5. In America, many of our children are still "couch potatoes," which is a slang term for television addict. This not only steals much of their time during some potentially great learning years, but it also damages their bodies, both by promoting physical inactivity, and by promoting high-fat low-fiber "foods." Try to stimulate them and their families toward more productive things, such as music, sports, reading, and family devotions.

6. Children need good role models, and that should be part of a good Sunday School teacher's job. Take care of your own body. Stay in shape and in good health by eating right and exercising. This will encourage them in that area more than lectures.

Intellectual Development

1. Fifth graders should be good readers. By now, they should be able to at least read along with the group. Be careful, however, about singling out individuals to read. Some are weak readers and will be very embarrassed.

2. They can memorize easily, and are probably capable of more than you think. Their minds are clear, and ready to receive.

3. They are beginning to grasp some abstract concepts, but still will have trouble thinking in analogies. Be clear and precise, and try to communicate, because analogies are extremely important to understanding the Bible.

4. If challenged and given a little instruction, fifth graders could probably write poems, or even songs. Even though their creativity may be somewhat dam-

aged by overexposure to television or sensual music, they still have potential. Give them opportunities to be creative in a positive way. Why not challenge the class in a poetry, story, or song-writing contest?

5. By now, they should know some Bible, or at least know the books of the Bible in order. Have a periodic drill on the books of the Bible, and challenge them to correlate known Scripture passages with life situations. Start them thinking and participating.

6. Ask questions, and show respect for them when they give wrong ansers. However, do not treat their answers as if they were right, because you could cause confusion. Point out any right concepts, but gently lead them to the Word of God and right doctrine.

7. Fifth graders greatly need role models. Emphasize the biographies of great Christians, and encourage them to read good books.

Social Development

1. On the average, fifth graders are moving toward more group loyalty and away from a family focus. We do not consider this good, and will try to stand against peer-orientation that is strongly affecting children in our society. Encourage them to trust and talk to their parents. Encourage the parents to communicate and spend quality time with their children. Let the parents know you are there to support and help them in their role as the primary spiritual leaders of their children.

2. They still prefer the "pals" of their own gender, but that is beginning to change. The girls are already

very aware of boys, but the boys are not noticing the girls. Some girls may be "boy-crazy," and, as a rule, that is not healthy. Lead them away from the dating mentality they are exposed to so often, and toward a healthy Biblical view that they should be friends with one another and act like caring brothers and sisters. Play down the gender emphasis.

Some churches have found this to be a good age to have separate classes for boys and girls. They can then focus on ways to strengthen proper social responses that are characteristic of their gender. Girls can focus on poise and beauty, and boys can learn about manners and social skills.

3. They are very concerned with "fairness." Teach them the difference between fairness and justice, and show the values and benefits we can gain if we respond with a right attitude to the many "unfair" situations in life. Teach them to "prefer one another in love" instead of trying to get "their fair share" in life. Show them that the life message of Jesus was that "it is more blessed to give than to receive."

4. The boys may be self-conscious, especially about praise and worship. They will want to appear "cool," and be hesitant about singing. Remember that self-consciousness is an evidence of a lack of God-consciousness, so help them to get close to God, and to learn the fear of the Lord. Show them that a healthy response to God in singing is an evidence of strength, and that their silence is the result of fear, not maturity.

Spiritual Development

1. Fifth graders who have been in Sunday School for several years, have heard many lessons and many appeals for salvation. It is important for the teacher to be aware of the spiritual condition of the students and of their Christian background, or lack of it. If there are some unsaved young people in the group, there will be times which are conducive for an "altar call," or at least a question about their spiritual condition to be followed up later. If only one or two children have not made a confession of faith, rather than single them out and focus the entire group on their need, why not meet with them or their family later, and lead them to the Lord? It would probably be much more meaningful to them, and would prevent a few possible problems.

If we have an altar call every week for **"churched"** children,

a. They will tend to develop the idea that the salvation experience is all there is to Sunday School, and not keep a learner's heart later on. They may be more likely to drop out, with the idea that "I already got saved; several times, in fact. I don't need to go back."

b. There will be an embarrassing focus on one or two who are known to be new or unsaved.

c. We will miss opportunities to lead them to other experiences or character development. This is a good age for them to receive the baptism in the Holy Spirit, or to learn serving and giving.

d. It will get to be a ritual (rut), and lose its effectiveness.

Listen to the Holy Spirit to know when to make a spiritual appeal for salvation.

2. The spirits of fifth graders are able to respond to spiritual truths, but perhaps their minds cannot fully grasp them yet. Use analogies and keep teaching and praying. The Holy Spirit is able to make truth come alive in their spirits and their understanding.

3. They should understand the purpose and significance of water baptism, and should be thoroughly taught and encouraged to be buried in the waters of Christian baptism.

4. They need to be led and encouraged to respond in the Spirit, and not just focus on the social and intellectual aspects of life and religion. They should be able to hear from God and respond to Him.

A Profile of Sixth Grade Students

Physical Development

1. They are healthy and growing. Some of the boys are beginning to catch up with the girls, and to develop more physical strength so that they are not as equal in athletic activities.

2. Their motor skills are greater now then ever, and they should be learning some artistic skills. The voices of the boys have not changed yet. Their range should be higher than in previous years. They are more able to sing in the adult ranges, but without the bass section.

3. Most of the girls are going through puberty, but most the boys are not. This can have an effect on them emotionally, especially in a culture that flaunts sen-

suality and promotes a preoccupation with sex. They are extremely self-conscious, and need to be challenged to focus on character and spiritual maturity.

Today, young people go through puberty at an earlier age than previous generations. Some health professionals have attributed this to our increased use of steriods and other stimulants in livestock, and to our high-fat and protein diet. Whatever the cause, the early development of an adult body is not good for children's development. It shortens their childhood, and thrusts them into pressures and temptations for which they are not ready. While there is social pressure on them to try to look like adults and get caught up in the emotionally devasting dating game, it is far wiser to encourage them to be active in sports, music, academics, and group activities which do not emphasize their gender.

4. Unlike most previous generations, American young people usually have little demand placed on them for physical work. This sedentary lifestyle is a constant temptation, and coupled with the American fat-sugar diet, can be very damaging to physical health and well-being. Teenagers need regular physical exercise, and they need to learn physical disciplines that will benefit them for life. *"For bodily exercise profiteth little: but godliness is profitable unto all things" (I Timothy 4:8).*

Intellectual Development

1. Sixth graders have a keen mind and can retain information and memorize much more quickly than they will likely be able to when they are adults. Do not underestimate their abilities. Challenge their

minds and do not talk down to them. They do not know as much as they think they do, but they have clear minds (unless they have already damaged them with drugs). Remember that the humanist educators believe in evolution, and often tell students, "You are smarter than your parents." This is often implied, and sometimes directly stated.

As Christian teachers, we need to reinforce the relationship with parents, and encourage respect for godly authority and the wisdom of years. It is amazing how Hollywood and the entertainment world consistently portray parents and teachers as wrong, stupid, and uncaring, while children are portrayed as intellectually superior. This is part of the humanist's philosophy. The secular agenda is to encourage everyone to "be his own person" and reject authority, since "there is no absolute authority (God)."

2. They can memorize easily, so challenge them to fill their minds with wisdom and that which has eternal value.

3. They are less inclined to hero worship and more involved with visualizing or fantasizing themselves as heroes. They greatly need self-esteem, and should have an abundance of hope for their future.

4. If they watch much secular television and attend a secular school, they will tend to have a mindset that is focused on temporal values, with little thought for God and eternity. Some of the ideas being promoted by humanism are: "Be your own person." "Life just happens (evolution)." "The purpose of life is to be happy, successful, and free." "If it feels good, do it."

As a Christian teacher, be aware that you need to combat "the lie" and promote a Christian world view in your life and teaching. Let your students know that: "You are not your own, you are bought with a price." "God is in control and has a specific plan for your life. The purpose of life is to respond and relate to God, and to please Him as a servant." "Real freedom is freedom from sin, not freedom from authority." "If it pleases God, do it."

5. They are probably fairly confident as "top dogs" in the elementary world. They should know the books of the Bible and many stories and scripture passages. One danger teachers have here is to make the Bible too simple and repetitious. They are starting to grasp abstract concepts and analogies; so, focus on them, and do not be afraid to talk over their heads occassionally. They need to see that the Bible is deep and exciting, and that it consists of more than a few simplistic stories with one-dimensional messages. They need a sense of awe about God. In fact, there is a serious lack of the fear of the Lord. So, teach sound doctrine and eschatology.

6. They need to be challenged and stimulated to participate in discussions, and should be especially encouraged to ask questions about the lesson. You know you are keeping their interest if you are stimulating honest questions. Also, do not be afraid to say, "I do not know, but I will try to find out this week." They are capable of some baffling questions.

Social Development

1. On the average, sixth graders are moving toward more group loyalty and away from a family focus. We do not consider this good, and will try to stand against the peer-orientation that is strongly

affecting children in our society. Encourage them to trust and talk to their parents. Encourage the parents to communicate and spend quality time with their children. Let the parents known you are there to support and help them in their role as the primary spiritual leaders of their children.

2. They still prefer the "pals" of their own gender, but that is beginning to change. The girls are already very aware of boys, but the boys are not noticing. Some girls may be "boy-crazy," and, as a rule, that is not healthy. Lead them away from the dating mentality they are exposed to so often, and toward a healthy Biblical view that they should be friends with one another and act like caring brothers and sisters. Play down the gender emphasis.

3. They are very concerned with "fairness." Teach them the difference between fairness and justice, and show the values and benefits we can gain if we respond with a right attitude to the many "unfair" situations in life. Teach them to "prefer one another in love" instead of trying to get "their fair share" in life. Show them that the life message of Jesus was that "it is more blessed to give than to receive."

4. The boys may be self-conscious, especially about praise and worship. They will want to appear "cool," and be hesitant about singing. Remember that self-consciousness is an evidence of a lack of God-consciousness, so help them to get close to God, and to learn the fear of the Lord. Show them that a healthy response to God in singing is an evidence of strength, and that their silence is the result of fear, not maturity.

5. This is a time for intense peer pressure toward conformity. They have been involved in peer group training for years, and are naturally identifying more and more with peers and moving away from family loyalty and dependence. If they do not have a strong sense of self-esteem and purpose, developed in a strong, loving family structure, they will tend to be very insecure and desperate for peer acceptance. They may have a great fear of being different. Teach them the values of standing alone against evil, and a values system based on eternity.

Spiritual Development

1. The sixth grade is a critical time to establish children in a spiritual foundation and a Christian world view. Many of them know the Word, and are able to understand spirtually almost as much as the adults, but they usually have few opportunities for spiritual ministry. They need to realize that they still have much to learn and should respect and honor their parents and teachers. They should also be encouraged to take spiritual responsibility and to participate in the work of soul-winning, worship and service.

2. This is a time of spiritual warfare. The world is making an intense effort to capture the minds and hearts of our children with the allure of temporal values. Many youth leaders today make the mistake of trying to communicate the message, "You can be saved and still party and have a good time." That is close; but, remember that we can never compete with the world on the flesh level. That is their turf. Our message should be, "You can enjoy the Lord and the

things of the Spirit. When you delight yourself in the Lord, the phony, substitute pleasures of the world will not compare with genuine, spiritual joy. *Proverbs 22:6 says, "Train up a child in the way he should go and when he is old he will not depart from it."* In other words, cultivate a taste for the Spirit in a child and teach him to live for eternity, instead of for the moment. Then, as he grows he will not have to "sow his wild oats" and then reap a harvest of heartache.

3. They need to minister to the Lord in worship and to minister to one another in prayer, exhorting and service. Do not do all the ministering for them, and do not just sing songs to make music. Teach them to enter into God's presence, and teach them to share a good, edifying testimony. Encourage them to work together in ministry projects where they give to people in need. Make sure their goals are not always centered in fun trips and parties.

4. Their spirits are able to respond to spiritual truths that perhaps their minds are not able to grasp yet. Use analogies and pray for the anointing. Remember that the greatest teacher who ever lived was constantly appealing to the spirits of His listeners, knowing that their minds did not grasp much of what He said.

5. They need to be led and encouraged to respond to the Holy Spirit, and not just to the music and social interaction. They have a tendency at this age to get caught up in a focus on themselves and one another, and to see church activity as more social than spiritual.

A Profile of Seventh Grade Students

Physical Development

1. The growth rate of seventh graders is rapid. Boys may grow as much as 4" in height in a year.

2. Girls mature earlier than boys, both physically and emotionally. This results in times of embarrassment and awkwardness in their responses to one another.

3. They are going through puberty, the time that their bodies make the transition from childhood to adulthood. This can have a traumatic effect on them emotionally, especially in a culture that flaunts sensuality and promotes a preoccupation with sex. They are extremely self-conscious, and need to be challenged to focus on character and spiritual maturity.

Today, young people go through puberty at an earlier age than previous generations. Some health professionals have attributed this to our increased use of steriods and other stimulants in livestock, and to our high-fat and protein diet. Whatever the cause, the early development of an adult body is not good for children's development. It shortens their childhood, and thrusts them into pressures and temptations for which they are not ready. While there is social pressure on them to try to look like adults and get caught up in the emotionally devasting dating game, it is far wiser to encourage them to be active in sports, music, academics, and group activities which do not emphasize their gender.

4. Unlike most previous generations, American young people usually have little demand placed on

them for physical work. This sedentary lifestyle is a constant temptation, and coupled with the American fat-sugar diet, can be very damaging to physical health and well-being. Teenagers need regular physical exercise, and they need to learn physical disciplines that will benefit them for life. *"For bodily exercise profiteth little: but godliness is profitable unto all things" (I Timothy 4:8).*

5. They are quick to become frustrated or dissatisfied with their physical appearance, as the world stimulates a focus on outward appearance and relates acceptance and acceptability to physical beauty. Teach them godly self-acceptance, and teach them to focus on inward character, not just outward beauty. It may be good to teach them to take care of their bodies, but not to the point of preoccupation with self. *"Whose adorning let it not be that outward adorning...but let it be the hidden man of the heart...even the ornament of a meek and quiet spirit " (I Peter 3:3-4).*

Intellectual Development

1. Seventh graders have a keen mind and can retain information and memorize much more quickly than they will likely be able to when they are adults. Do not underestimate their abilities. Challenge their minds and do not talk down to them. They do not know as much as they think they do, but they have clear minds (unless they have already damaged them with drugs). Remember that the humanist educators believe in evolution and often tell students, "You are smarter than your parents." This is often implied, and sometimes directly stated. As Christian teachers, we

need to reinforce the relationship with parents, and encourage respect for godly authority and the wisdom of years. It is amazing how Hollywood and the entertainment world consistently portray parents and teachers as wrong, stupid, and uncaring, while children are portrayed as intellectually superior. This is part of the humanist's philosophy. The secular agenda is to encourage everyone to "be his own person" and reject authority, since "there is no absolute authority (God)."

2. They can memorize easily, so challenge them to fill their minds with wisdom and that which has eternal value.

3. They are less inclined to hero worship and more involved with visualizing or fantasizing themselves as heroes. They greatly need self-esteem, and should have an abundance of hope for their future.

4. If they watch much secular television and attend a secular school, they will tend to have a mindset that is focused on temporal values, with little thought for God and eternity. Some of the ideas being promoted by humanism are: "Be your own person." "Life just happens (evolution)." "The purpose of life is to be happy, successful, and free." "If it feels good, do it."

As a Christian teacher, be aware that you need to combat "the lie" and promote a Christian world view in your life and teaching. Let your students know that: "You are not your own, you are bought with a price." "God is in control and has a specific plan for your life. The purpose of life is to respond and relate to God, and to please Him as a servant." "Real freedom is freedom from sin, not freedom from authority." "If it pleases God, do it."

5. They can daydream easily, so you are challenged to gain and hold their attention. Just because their eyes are pointed toward you does not mean their brains are anywhere in the same room, or planet. While imagination is healthy, fantasy can be extremely dangerous. When influenced with the secular "power" fantasies that are popular in the world, a fantasy dream world can contribute to depression, confusion, rebellion, mental suicide (drugs), moral suicide (promiscuity), physical self-destruction.

Understand the difference between fantasy and vision. Vision relates to hope and faith. Without a (spiritual) vision people perish (become wild and undisciplined). Children need to be stimulated in a healthy imagination. To "pretend" and play is a major part of their development. They are able to begin to understand that there is a supernatural realm in God's creation, and that angels and demons are real.

Fantasy is a satanic counterfeit to vision. Fantasy focuses on inaccessible and impossible dreams that exalt the dreamer and feeds off the selfish ego tendencies of the sin nature. There is much emphasis on "power" and self-glory. Today there is avalanche of fantasy material ready to pour into the minds of children through television, humanistic books, and movies. The character seem "good" and "so cute," but the message is demonic. Fantasy opens the mind to the occult and often leads to confusion, rebellion, depression, and suicide.

Social Development

1. This is a time for intense peer pressure toward conformity. Seventh graders have been involved in

peer group training for years, and are naturally identifying more and more with peers and moving away from family loyalty and dependence. If they do not have a strong sense of self-esteem and purpose, developed in a strong, loving family structure, they will tend to be very insecure and desperate for peer acceptance. They will have a great fear of being different. There is a great focus on fads and temporal values.

2. If they are self-centered in their thinking, they will tend to be peer-centered in their quest for self-esteem. They need to develop a healthy sense of self-acceptance by drawing their identity from their relationship to God and their families.

3. This can be a time for great insecurity as they make the transition from grade school to junior high. In their minds, it can be equated with moving from childhood to adulthood, with its increased demands and pressures. If they are in a traditional school setting, then they are no longer in the security of a one-classroom, one-teacher nest. They may see on television that people their age are portrayed as more mature and intelligent than adults, and that puts impossible expectations on them. It also tends to alienate them from authority figures at a time when they need them the most. Be careful to avoid the adult expectation "be your own person" mentality. Let them be a child who is growing and discovering naturally; not one who is thrust into an adult world overnight. Try to strengthen the bond with their parents and emphasize the value and safety in being under authority.

4. Seventh graders will have a tendency to transfer their loyalties to their peer group or carnal "heroes" and away from parents and godly role models.

As teachers, we want to reinforce the God-ordained bond of family, and help to "turn the hearts of...children to their fathers." Focus on Christian biographies, and teach them to look at the character and influence of their entertainment "heroes," and not just at their beauty, wealth, and rhythm.

5. They will tend to "follow the crowd" and to form cliques. It is healthy to form close friendships with a few people, and to have a "best friend," but only if those relationships influence the members positively toward God. A group with a sensual or rebellious focus will be devastating. *"He that walketh with wise men shall be wise, but a companion of fools shall be destroyed" (Proverbs 13:20).*

Spiritual Development

1. The seventh grade is a critical time to establish students in a spiritual foundation and a Christian world view. Many of them know the Word, and are able to understand spiritually almost as much as the adults, but they usually have few opportunities for spiritual ministry. They need to realize that they still have much to learn and should respect and honor their parents and teachers. They should also be encouraged to take spiritual responsibility and to participate in the work of soul-winning, worship, and service.

2. This is a time of spiritual warfare. The world is making an intense effort to capture the minds and hearts of our children with the allure of temporal values. Many youth leaders today make the mistake of trying to communicate the message, "You can be saved and still party and have a good time." That is

close; but, remember that we can never compete with the world on the flesh level. That is their turf. Our message should be, "You can enjoy the Lord and things of the Spirit. When you delight yourself in the Lord, the phony, substitute pleasures of the world will not compare with genuine, spiritual joy. ***Proverbs 22:6 says, "Train up a child in the way he should go and when he is old he will not depart from it."*** In other words, cultivate a taste for the Spirit in a child and teach him to live for eternity, instead of for the moment. Then, as he grows he will not have to "sow his wild oats" and then reap a harvest of heartache.

3. They need to minister to the Lord in worship and to minister to one another in prayer, exhorting, and service. Do not do all the ministering for them, and do not just sing songs to make music. Teach them to enter into God's presence, and teach them to share a good, edifying testimony. Encourage them to work together in ministry projects where they give to people in need. Make sure their goals are not always centered in fun trips and parties.

4. Some of our most common mistakes with Junior High Youth:

a. We try too hard to keep them with entertainment and fail to stimulate their spirit enough.

b. We fail to use or stimulate their ability to function in the spiritual realm.

c. We allow them to delight themselves and love (worship) secular herioes, hoping that they will choose for themselves the right examples.

d. We tend to allow too much exposure to evil. The Bible teaches us to do as much good and as little evil as possible. *"For my people...are wise to do evil, but to do good they have no knowledge" (Jeremiah 4:22).*

A Profile of Eighth Grade Students

Physical Development

1. The growth rate of eighth graders is rapid. Boys may grow as much as 6" in height in a year.

2. Girls mature earlier than boys, both physically and emotionally. This results in times of embarrassment and awkwardness in their responses to one another.

3. They are going through puberty, the time that their bodies make the transition from childhood to adulthood. This can have a traumatic effort on them emotionally, especially in a culture that flaunts sensuality and promotes a preoccupation with sex. They are extremely self-conscious, and need to be challenged to focus on character and spiritual maturity.

Today, young people go through puberty at an earlier age than previous generations. Some health professionals have attributed this to our increased use of steroids and other stimulants in livestock, and to our high-fat and protein diet. Whatever the cause, the early development of an adult body is not good for children's development. It shortens their childhood, and thrusts them into pressures and temptations for which they are not ready. While there is social pressure on them to try to look like adults and get caught up in the emotionally devastating dating game, it is far wiser to encourage them to be active in sports, music, academics, and group activities which do not emphasize their gender.

4. Unlike most previous generations, American young people usually have little demand placed on them for physical work. This sedentary lifestyle is a constant temptation, and coupled with the American fat-sugar diet, can be very damaging to physical health and well-being. Teenagers need regular physical exercise, and they need to learn physical disciplines that will benefit them for life. ***"For bodily exercise profiteth little: but godliness is profitable unto all things" (I Timothy 4:8).***

5. They are quick to become frustrated or dissatisfied with their physical appearance, as the world stimulates a focus on outward appearance and relates acceptance and acceptability to physical beauty. Teach them godly self-acceptance, and teach them to focus on inward character, not just outward beauty. It may be good to teach them to take care of their bodies, but not to the point of preoccupation with self. ***"Whose adorning let it not be that outward adorning...but let it be the hidden man of the heart...even the ornament of a meek and quiet spirit" (I Peter 3:3-4).***

Intellectual Development

1. Eighth graders have a keen mind and can retain information and memorize much more quickly than they will likely be able to when they are adults. Do not underestimate their abilities. Challenge their minds and do not talk down to them. They do not know as much as they think they do, but they have clear minds (unless they have already damaged them

with drugs). Remember that the humanist educators believe in evolution, and often tell students, "You are smarter than your parents." This is often implied, and sometimes directly stated.

As Christian teachers, we need to reinforce the relationship with parents, and encourage respect for Godly authority and the wisdom of years. It is amazing how Hollywood and the entertainment world consistently portray parents and teachers as wrong, stupid, and uncaring, while children are portrayed as intellectually superior. This is part of the humanist's philosophy. The secular agenda is to encourage everyone to "be his own person" and reject authority, since "there is no absolute authority (God)."

2. They can memorize easily, so challenge them to fill their minds with wisdom and that which has eternal value.

3. They are less inclined to hero worship and more involved with visualizing or fantasizing themselves as heroes. They greatly need self-esteem, and should have an abundance of hope for their future.

4. If they watch much secular television and attend a secular school, they will tend to have a mindset that is focused on temporal values, with little thought for God and eternity. Some of the ideas being promoted by humanism are: "Be your own person." "Life just happens (evolution)." "The purpose of life is to be happy, successful, and free." "If it feels good, do it."

As a Christian teacher, be aware that you need to combat "the lie" and promote a Christian world view in your life and teaching. Let your students know that: "You are not your own, you are bought with a price." "God is in control and has a specific plan for your life. The purpose of life is to respond and relate to God, and to please Him as a servant." "Real freedom is freedom from sin, not freedom from authority." "If it pleases God, do it."

5. They can daydream easily, so you are challenged to gain and hold their attention. Just because their eyes are pointed toward you does not mean their brains are anywhere in the same room, or planet. While imagination is healthy, fantasy can be extremely dangerous. When influenced with the secular "power" fantasies that are popular in the world, a fantasy dream world can contribute to depression, confusion, rebellion, mental suicide (drugs), moral suicide (promiscuity), and physical self-destruction.

Understand the difference between fantasy and vision. Vision relates to hope and faith. Without a (spiritual) vision people perish (become wild and undisciplined). Children need to be stimulated in a healthy imagination. To "pretend" and play is a major part of their development. They are able to begin to understand that there is a supernatural realm in God's creation, and that angels and demons are real.

Fantasy is a satanic counterfeit to vision. Fantasy focuses on inaccessible and impossible dreams that exalt the dreamer and feeds off the selfish ego tendencies of the sin nature. There is much emphasis on "power" and self-glory. Today there is an avalanche of fantasy material ready to pour into the minds of children through television, humanistic books, and movies. The characters seem "good" and "so cute," but the message is demonic. Fantasy opens the mind to the occult and often leads to confusion, rebellion, depression, and suicide.

Social Development

1. This is a time for intense peer pressure toward conformity. Seventh graders have been involved in peer group training for years, and are naturally identifying more and more with their peers and moving away from family loyalty and dependence. If they do not have a strong sense of self-esteem and purpose, developed in a strong, loving family structure, they will tend to be very insecure and desperate for peer acceptance. They will have a great fear of being different. There is a great focus on fads and temporal values.

2. If they are self-centered in their thinking, they will tend to be peer-centered in their quest for self-esteem. They need to develop a healthy sense of self-acceptance by drawing their identity from their relationship to God and their families.

3. Girls are very conscious of boys, and the boys are beginning to notice. They boys are dropping out of the "girl-hater, confirmed bachelor" clubs, and are grudgingly admitting, after awhile, that girls are "OK," sometimes. There will be great social pressure to get caught up in the dating game. This sets them up for devastating blows to their self-esteem, as each has a focus on being liked and accepted, instead of a focus on being a friend and a servant to others. The wisdom of Scripture can prevent this. Young men are told to *treat the younger women as sisters.* In other words, be a friend, and have fun in a group without a selfish focus on possessing anyone.

4. Eighth graders will have a tendency to transfer their loyalties to their peer group or carnal "heroes" and away from parents and godly role models. As

teachers, we want to reinforce the God-ordained bond of family, and help to "turn the hearts of...children to their fathers." Focus on Christian biographies, and teach them to look at the character and influence of their entertainment "heroes," and not just at their beauty, wealth, and rhythm.

5. They will tend to "follow the crowd" and to form cliques. It is healthy to form close friendships with a few people, and to have a "best friend," but only if those relationships influence the member positively toward God. A group with a sensual or rebellious focus will be devastating. *"He that walketh with wise men shall be wise, but a companion of fools shall be destroyed" (Proverbs 13:20).*

Spiritual Development

1. The eighth grade is a critical time for young people to establish themselves in a spiritual foundation and a Christian world view. Many of them know the Word, and are able to understand spiritually almost as much as the adults, but they usually have few opportunities for spiritual ministry. They need to realize that they still have much to learn and should respect and honor their parents and teachers. They should also be encouraged to take spiritual responsibility and to participate in the work of soul-winning, worship, and service.

2. This is a time of spiritual warfare. The world is making an intense effort to capture the minds and hearts of our children with the allure of temporal values. Many youth leaders today make the mistake of trying to communicate the message, "You can be saved and still party and have a good time." That is

close; but, remember that we can never compete with the world on the flesh level. That is their turf. Our message should be, "You can enjoy the Lord and the things of the Spirit. When you delight yourself in the Lord, the phony, substitute pleasures of the world will not compare with genuine, spiritual joy." *Proverbs 22:6 says, "Train up a child in the way he should go and when he is old he will not depart from it."* In other words, cultivate a taste for the Spirit in a child and teach him to live for eternity, instead of for the moment. Then, as he grows, he will not have to "sow his wild oats" and then reap a harvest of heartache.

3. They need to minister to the Lord in worship and to minister to one another in prayer, exhorting, and service. Do not do all the ministering for them, and do not just sing songs to make music. Teach them to enter into God's presence, and teach them to share a good, edifying testimony. Encourage them to work together in ministry projects where they give to people in need. Make sure their goals are not always centered in fun trips and parties.

4. Some of our most common mistakes with Junior High youth:

a. We try too hard to keep them with entertainment and fail to stimulate their spirit enough.

b. We fail to use or stimulate their ability to function in the spiritual realm.

c. We allow them to delight themselves and love (worship) secular heroes, hoping that they will choose for themselves the right examples.

d. We tend to allow too much exposure to evil. The Bible teaches us to do as much good and as little evil as possible. *"For my people...are wise to do evil, but to do good they have no knowledge" (Jeremiah 4:22).*

A Profile of 9th and 10th Grade Students
Physical Development

1. For many teenagers, the awkward and often turbulent journey through puberty is near completion. By the 9th or 10th grade, most teenagers "catch up" with their peers in physical development. During this time, it is important to understand that teenagers are very concerned with their physical appearance and apparel. Such ordinary problems as a facial blemish or not having the right brand of clothing may seem trivial to an adult; but, to a teenager, it is a brutal blow to self-esteem. We need to be aware of this, and emphasize that God made us the way we are for a purpose. He is more concerned with the development of our inner character (I Samuel 16:7) than physical beauty which is temporal (Proverbs 31:30).

2. Teenagers are extremely aware of their sexual development, and sexual experimentation often begins during this time. We need to have our guns loaded when a teenager asks, "What's wrong with premarital sex?"

3. Teenagers frequently develop an erroneous sense of being indestructible. Many may experiment with drugs and alcohol, out of curiosity or peer pressure, with the thought that it will not effect them. It is important that we teach teenagers that their body is the temple of the Holy Spirit, and that they should

is the temple of the Holy Spirit, and that they should honor God with their body by taking care of it (I Corinthians 6:19).

4. Teenagers may have unpredictable mood swings. Emotions are strong and fragile. One minute they are skipping and singing, but in a short time they may be angry or depressed. It is important that we recognize this in teenagers. Be willing to weather the storm with them.

Intellectual Development

1. It is during the 9th and 10th grades that youth move from concrete thinking to abstract thinking. They begin to experience a new world of ideas and concepts. They do not take beliefs at face value anymore, but begin to question and inquire. With younger children, a teacher may be very effective with storytelling; however, as cognitive thinking develops, it is important to use interactive learning, such as panel and group discussions, questions and answers, debates and symposiums.

2. We live in an instant entertainment society. The average teenager watches between 3 and 5 hours of television a day and listens to music from 4 to 6 hours a day. Many teenagers go to sleep with music playing. Teenagers are overexposed, but underdeveloped. We must challenge them to use their intellect. The mind, like a muscle, must be used in order to grow stronger. The mind of the typical American teenager, with its diet of TV, VCR, and CD's, is jello. *We must challenge teenagers to think!*

Teenagers should be challenged to memorize Scripture. They are now capable of memorizing long passages of Scripture, even chapters.

Teenagers should be challenged to read. Teenagers who develop good reading habits have the world at their fingertips (Proverbs 4:7).

Teenagers should be challenged to write. Why do teenagers dislike essay tests and writing assignments in school? It is because writing takes thinking ---- the organization of thoughts ---- something with which many American teenagers are unaccustomed. Teenagers should not be spoon-fed all the answers. The mistake we make is that we often tell teenagers what to think, instead of teaching them how to think. If teenagers ask a question concerning evolution, then encourage them to do research, direct them to some good materials on the subject, but do not ramble through 100 proofs for creationism immediately. Challenge them to think for themselves. Remember, if the mind is not worked, then, like a muscle, it will be weak.

3. Creativity begins to grow. We need to give teenagers the opportunity to express themselves through such learning activities as problem-solving and role-playing. Encouraging teenagers in art and drama is also an effective way to spark creativity.

4. Teenagers begin to make decisions on their own. It is important that we help them make wise decisions by encouraging them to look at the possibilities and consider the consequences.

Social Development

1. Friends are life. The social development of teenagers at this age begins to take dominance. Peer groups or cliques are forming. The high school cafeteria is divided into various peer clusters such as jocks, headbangers, preppies, ethnic minorities, etc. All adolescents are influenced by their peers, and many teenagers will do almost anything to be accepted by their peer group. It is important that we teach teenagers the qualities of courage and conviction. Teenagers should also be challenged to be "other-centered" (Philippians 2:3, 4) and reach out to those around them. It should be noted that, if a teenager does not make friends within the youth group, chances are good that the teenager will not stick around and will begin to look for friends elsewhere. We must provide enjoyable activities that encourage teenagers to get acquainted with each other. Class crowd-breakers, group projects, and social activities are good places to sow seeds for building friendships.

2. During this time, teenagers begin to struggle for independence with parents. Teenagers want the freedom to do as they please: yet, they are not capable, emotionally or economically, of handling the responsibility of living without their parents. It is a difficult experience for both teenagers and parents. A questionable party away from home rarely excites the parents, and a quiet evening with the folks rarely excites the teenagers. Often, we must encourage youth to communicate with their parents, and we have the responsibility to share the importance of parental obedience.

3. The teenager's interest in the opposite sex is high. It is a time when boys and girls begin to communicate their interest in one another. Boys become "girl scouts" and vice versa. We need to provide a positive social atmosphere so that healthy friendships between the sexes can develop. Too often in our society, teenagers become lovers before they become friends. We need to emphasize the importance of Biblical friendship (I Timothy 5:2), and we need to provide opportunities for social interaction.

Spiritual Development

1. At this age, teenagers start to question their faith. As they develop intellectually, teenagers begin to search for adequate reasons for faith. Do they believe, because their parents told them to; or, do they believe because it is truth? As they develop socially, they may have friends at school with different beliefs. How do they know whether or not what they believe is true? It is important to understand that doubt does not necessarily mean danger. We are to love the Lord with all our *"mind" (Matthew 22:37)*. We cannot love the Lord with all our mind if we do not use it. Doubt can lead to a careful examination of beliefs, which often leads to a more personal, firsthand acceptance of the tenets of faith. Although this experience can give parents an anxiety attack, "Lord! Save my child!", with patience and prayer, it may ultimately strengthen the teenager's faith. Remember, the challenge of the Bible is: *"Taste and see that the Lord is good..." (Psalm 34:8)*. At this stage in their development, teenagers need more than being told, they need to taste.

2. Teenagers are open to spiritual concerns. Although teenagers may question what they believe, this does not mean they are uninterested in God or religious matters. It is critical that we give a clear presentation of the gospel. Teenagers will respond to the claims of Christ!

3. We must show teenagers how their faith can relate to their daily living. Church becomes irrelevant when the teenager sees no connection between what happens during the week and what is taught in church on Sunday. We must show how living by Biblical principles will lead to a satisfying and rewarding life (I Peter 3:10).

A Profile of 11th and 12th Grade Students

Physical Development

1. By this time, except for an occasional "late bloomer," the journey through puberty is complete. The body has filled out; the voice has changed, and growth spurt has ended. Physically, the teenager may be considered an adult. Usually, at this time, teenagers begin to accept their physcial appearance and are concerned with good hygiene and fitness. They may start a serious weightlifting or exercise program. It is important to understand that while physical maturity has fully developed, emotional maturity is a slower process, and although they may look grown-up, they may not always act grown-up. The key word for working with teenagers is "patience."

2. If a teenager is still a virgin at this age, then the pressure to have sex escalates. We must continue

to stress the importance of setting Biblical standards for physical expression. God's way is the best way.

3. By this time, a teenager who earlier experimented with drugs and alcohol, may become a regular user and an eventual addict. This tragedy often comes to the forefront in a crisis situation. The teenager is caught or crashes while driving drunk. The teenager is busted for buying or selling drugs. The teenager is hospitalized from an overdose. It is important to have competent counseling resources with which to help the teenager.

4. The extreme highs and lows of emotion usually pass by this age. Feelings become more controlled, although an occasional outburst is still to be expected. We must continue to give unconditional love and support.

Intellectual Development

1. Their cognitive abilities and mental capacities continue to expand. Their concentration and attention span increases. Teenagers begin to relate to adults on an adult level. We must begin to treat them on a level where their views and opinions are respected. Our teaching must not be spoon-fed "me talk, you listen" exercises. It is important that dialogue and interaction take place in the teaching process. We must continually challenge them to think and discover truth for themselves.

2. During this time, teenagers begin to seek answers to serious questions in life, such as "Who am I?" What is the purpose of life?" "Why am I here?" It is imperative for us to instill a sense of destiny in

them by emphasizing that God has a plan and purpose for their lives (Jeremiah 29:11). This search for identity can be a tremendous opportunity for discipleship and spiritual growth as teenagers begin to get their eyes off the temporal and focus on the eternal.

3. School performance generally improves as teenagers begin to see the benefits of doing well academically, especially if they want to continue their education.

4. Decisions are being made that may effect them for the rest of their lives ---- decisions about furthering their education, decisions about career choices, decisions about relationships. We must give them insight for determining God's will during this critical time of life.

Social Development

1. During the 11th and 12th grades, the influence of peer pressure is not as dominant as in previous years. As social skills develop, and as personal interests and goals expand, the need for peer approval begins to diminish. They are developing an identity of their own. We should encourage them to reach out to others and befriend the younger teenagers within the youth group. This can have a very positive effect in building a sense of community in the youth ministry.

2. Teenagers are beginning to relate to adults on a peer level. Conversation and communication become more person-to-person than adult-to-child in content. We must treat them as adults.

3. During these last two years of high school, the struggle with parents over independence usually begins to diminish. Often, the teenager sees the need for parental help and guidance in selecting a college or vocation. Communication begins to improve. We can never overemphasize the importance of family relationships **(Ephesians 6:1-3).**

4. During this time, dating becomes important in the teenager's life. Thoughts of marriage may even enter the picture. Teenagers are becoming more skillful in relating to members of the opposite sex. We must continually stress the importance of developing healthy relationships and having self-control in the area of physical involvement.

Spiritual Development

1. During the 11th and 12th grades, many teenagers are sorting through their priorities and beliefs. They are searching for answers. Their questions should be addressed. They must be challenged spiritually. It is during this time that many teenagers make strong commitments to serve the Lord. We must challenge them to dedicate their lives to His service. Unfortunately, if teenagers are not significantly challenged, they may lose interest in spiritual matters after high school. This is our last chance to influence some of them positively for the cause of Christ.

2. Teenagers are very concerned about their future. Many are stepping out into the unknown for the first time. Their security is shaken. We must make them aware that God has a plan for their lives and

that true success and happiness comes from following Him.

3. We must continually present good role models to teenagers. In the long run, our character will do more for them than our Bible lessons. Adults who compromise, complain, and criticize are serious stumbling blocks for the spiritual growth of teenagers. We must be consistent examples.

Unless a teacher understands thoroughly the students in the class, they cannot be effective teachers. The ministry of the teaching is a high calling. **The Great Commission requires that the church be faithful in a teaching ministry.**

My prayer is that God will help you to do your very best, to recognize the **"MISSING ELEMENT"** in your church. Then, through **YOUR** proper planning and His empowerment, your church will **GROW!**.